Diversity, Educational Equity, & Learning Communities

Emily Lardner
with

Heather Keast
Barbara Williamson

Carol Hamilton
Jane Lister Reis

Phyllis van Slyck

Debora Barrera Pontillo
Catherine Crain

Charles Ryan Brown, Grace Dillon, Celine Fitzmaurice, Greg Jacob, Yves Labissiere, Antonia Levi, Cherry Muhanji, Candyce Reynolds, and Jack Straton

Learning Communities & Educational Reform

Summer 2005

Diversity, Educational Equity, and Learning Communities
Learning Communities & Educational Reform, Summer 2005

Contact Information
Washington Center for Improving the Quality of Undergraduate Education
The Evergreen State College
2700 Evergreen Parkway NW, SEM II E2115
Olympia, WA 98505
360.867.6611
360.867.6662 (fax)
www.evergreen.edu/washcenter
http://learningcommons.evergreen.edu

Recommended Bibliographic Listing
Lardner, E., with others. 2005. *Diversity, Educational Equity, and Learning Communities.* Learning Communities & Educational Reform, Summer. Olympia, WA: The Evergreen State College, Washington Center for Improving the Quality of Undergraduate Education.

Ordering Information
Additional copies of this publication may be ordered from:
The Evergreen State College Bookstore
2700 Evergreen Parkway NW
Olympia, WA 98505
360.867.5300
360.867.6793 (fax)

Reprint Permission

ISBN 1-56377-101-2

Contents

Acknowledgements

Thanks to the contributors to this monograph for their collaborative efforts to shape and give one another helpful advice during the writing and revising process. From the beginning, Patrick Hill has offered invaluable support on this project. Thanks also to Helen Fox at the University of Michigan for her careful reading and thoughtful comments, to Esmé Ryan for her editorial assistance, and to Dena Jaskar for layout and preparation of the final manuscript. Special recognition goes to Gillies Malnarich for her suggestions and thoughtful comments at various stages of this monograph.

Cover design and photo: Owen Freeman Additional photos: Sharilyn Howell

Preface

The deep purpose of education, in its best sense, is to support people in developing the capacity to live well together in the world. The ultimate measure of any educational reform effort will be the material changes we see in our communities. Such a transformation may not happen in our lifetimes, but the value of remembering the larger purpose for any reform effort is that like a constellation, also beyond reach, it helps us navigate a true course.

The learning community reform effort is a movement with promise, as many educators have noted. To make good on its full potential, we have to connect this powerful reform effort with the decades of work done primarily by scholars of color on issues of access and equity. Diversity is a demographic reality in the United States, and students in postsecondary education are increasingly diverse in terms of their ethnicities, races, socio-economic status, religions, ages, the languages spoken at home, physical abilities, countries of origin, and life experiences. In the mid-seventies, only about 15 percent of college students were members of minority groups. By 2000, the percentage of African American, Hispanic, Asian American, and Native American students had risen to 28 percent. But this fact of increasing diversity does not translate automatically into educational equity. Higher education in the United States continues to be marked by issues related to unequal access and retention—from the question of who even has a chance to begin to who completes their course of study. Moreover, focusing on improving access and retention alone doesn't translate automatically into making sure that all students have access to rich and rigorous curriculum.

Moving from the facts of diversity to the achievement of educational equity as measured by student learning and student academic achievement requires analysis, commitment, and sustained work at all levels. As a curriculum restructuring project, the learning community reform effort has a role to play in helping us achieve education equity. Nevertheless, in the absence of a clear analysis of who is served by the current learning community reform effort, as well as an analysis of the nature of the learning provided, this reform effort risks repeating the patterns of exclusion and segregation that characterize education overall and have for many years.

I grew up in Rock Island, Illinois, in the 1960s and 70s. My diverse town was racially segregated: most of the white families lived "up on the hill" and most of the African American families lived on the floodplain of the Mississippi River. I went to predominantly white schools. As a junior high school student, I participated in a cross-town exchange and spent a day at a racially-mixed school. Everything at this other school was different—clothes, voices, movements—and I realized that my "success" in one setting had little to do with negotiating social relations in this new setting. All public school students in my town eventually found themselves in a single consolidated high school. In 1973, race riots closed the high school for several days and the town was under a general curfew. Within the white community, rumors abounded about the possibility that busloads of Black Panthers were arriving from Chicago. My sister got into a fight in her gym class. My cousins and their friends drove to school with chains in the trunks of their cars. When school reopened, it was under the scrutiny of police and security guards who checked ID's and looked for weapons. In response to the tensions, high school administrators introduced a process called *Positive Peer Culture* (PPC) that had been developed in prisons for incarcerated youth. PPC is designed to mobilize the power of peer groups in a productive manner, by helping youth develop their collective abilities to identify problems and work toward their resolution.

When PPC was implemented at Rock Island High School, the goals for the program were to increase communication among students, reduce violence (especially fights), reduce racial prejudice, and lower the truancy rate. Student leaders and "problem youth" were recruited to form a racially-mixed group, which was facilitated by two African American men. As one of those student leaders, I found myself engaged in significant conversations with people whose life experiences and world-views were very different from mine—not only because of racial differences, but also because of class differences. Through our conversations, I became aware of the separate worlds within our high school—including the highly segregated academic and vocational tracks—as well as within our town. Supported by two extraordinary teachers, who encouraged us to listen and learn from each other and who believed that as a group we would figure out how the climate at our high school might be changed, we persevered in our conversations and efforts to appreciate the differences in our perspectives.

In spite of a wave of reforms, thirty years later the academic classes at my high school are still segregated. My parents reported that last spring there were no African American students enrolled in precalculus, and a disproportionately low number of students of color were honored at the Honors' Society Awards night. Schools across the nation report a similar academic achievement gap, at all levels. In spite of good intentions, in spite of three decades of efforts to respond to racial tensions, inequities remain. The lesson I draw from this is simple. We need to rethink our fundamental strategy for change. We need a deep shift from a charity-based model of social and educational change to a model based on justice. Charity-based models offer strategies to reduce the achievement gap—enrichment programs, bridge programs, scholarship programs. All are important. Nonetheless, we need to address the very causes that lead to educational inequities, and we must work on this collaboratively and consistently. Without a commitment to justice and to making sure that everyone has access to quality schools and to the living conditions that lead people to be ready and able to learn, educational equity is impossible. A genuine commitment to educational equity means acknowledging the importance of—and then working for—access to affordable and safe housing, ample and nutritious food, clean water, medical and dental care, and living-wage jobs for everyone. Unless we reverse the current social trends of privatizing social services and reducing public spending on basic rights, we will move further away from educational equity. The resources needed to address inequities found inside schools, which are exacerbated by deeper inequities outside of school, are not adequate, nor are the resources allocated for addressing the root causes.

Learning communities can help address inequities by educating citizens who have the knowledge, skills, and abilities to address our collective public and social issues. The purpose of this monograph is to integrate strategies drawn from decades of diversity work with the most current thinking about the elements leading to effective learning communities, the focus of the monograph's lead essay. The second section of the monograph consists of case stories from five campuses across the country that describe local efforts to bring the lessons of diversity work to bear on their learning community initiatives.

~ *Emily Lardner*

The Heart of Education: Translating Diversity into Equity

Emily Lardner

Achieving educational equity ultimately depends on changing conditions beyond school, including the factors that influence who is able to participate in postsecondary education. Learning communities can create powerful educational experiences for those who arrive at higher education, including the opportunity to develop the skills necessary for addressing social issues, including patterns of participation in postsecondary education. In 1927, John Dewey observed that "the public" has no hands—only individuals do. Consequently, only individuals acting together can address public problems. In Dewey's view, the aim of education in a democratic society is to help individuals develop the capacities to work together to solve public problems (104). Martin Luther King, Jr. makes a similar case, noting that addressing the complex issues facing our society requires stamina, persistence, and the determination to think problems through together, envisioning alternatives to the status quo (Washington 1986). As an exciting reform effort, learning communities provide a model of collaborative inquiry that students can use the rest of their lives. Throughout the curriculum, learning communities create opportunities for integrating learning across disciplines and developing knowledge and skills that can be used out in the world.

The term *learning communities* is used in widely different contexts, and learning communities serve a range of educational purposes. The term refers to a curricular reform strategy in postsecondary education aimed at creating or deepening students' experiences of being part of both a social and an academic community. Learning communities represent an alternative to the practice of taking a set of discrete courses taught by faculty who rarely know what their students are learning beyond the boundaries of the courses they are teaching. The assumption behind the discrete course model is that students will synthesize their own learning—for themselves and usually by themselves. Learning communities aim to make this process of integration an explicit part of students' experience. As well, in learning communities, students have opportunities to learn with and from others, so that they experience learning as a social, rather than an individual, process.

The spread of learning communities to more than 500 colleges and universities—two-year, four-year, public, and independent—is attributable in part to their widely documented effect on student retention and persistence (Tinto, Goodsell-Love, and Russo 1993; Taylor, et al. 2003). Learning communities are recognized as sites where student engagement can be fostered through a variety of means, including collaborative learning, community-based learning, and problem-based learning (Smith, MacGregor, et al. 2004; Levine Laufgraben, Shapiro, and Associates 2004; Eaton, MacGregor, and Schoem 2003; Smith 2001). As these writers point out, learning communities at their best represent a holistic response to developing more effective educational practices. Well-designed learning communities embody an analysis of the need to integrate learning, a theory of learning based on current research, a commitment to putting students at the center of our work in higher education, and a commitment to community as a necessary condition for learning (2004, 22). Because of the strong correlation between participating in learning communities and high levels of engagement, the National Survey of Student Engagement (NSSE), now includes "participating in a learning community" as one of the standard questions on the survey that goes to both first-year students and seniors.[1]

The advantages of encouraging students to make connections among the courses they are taking have been widely recognized. Capstone, thesis, and synthesis projects, and a host of other interdisciplinary projects are all intended to help students synthesize their learning. In *Beyond the Culture Wars* (1992), Gerald Graff argues that integrating learning across courses (and between the curriculum and the co-curriculum) is a powerful strategy for energizing students and faculty. Integration can occur, Graff notes, not only through formal learning communities, but also in a range of less formal practices. "Designing Integrated Learning" by Gillies Malnarich and Emily Lardner (2003), describes a methodology for helping faculty design integrated learning experiences regardless of the degree of connection among courses. Malnarich and Lardner outline a process to create a single linked assignment reflecting important shared learning outcomes. In many cases, students working on a linked assignment are not enrolled in the same courses but their professors create an opportunity for them to work with students in another course. Successful linked assignments frequently become the basis for more robust collaborations. Structured learning communities, with more formal links among courses, build upon these initial integrated assignments.

Although learning communities take different forms on different campuses, in general they refer to the practice of enrolling a group of students in two or more linked or clustered courses usually organized around an interdisciplinary theme or question. Currently, the most common learning community pattern on campuses is one where a cohort of students enrolls in a set of larger (usually unchanged) courses together, plus an additional integrative seminar. A second common pattern is that of linking or clustering courses. The same set of students enrolls in two or three courses, and the curriculum of the courses is integrated. Links or clusters are not usually fully team-taught. The third basic pattern is that of the coordinated studies program, in which a group of students enrolls in a set of fully integrated courses which are team-taught. A more detailed description of these three basic types of learning communities follows:

Small cohorts of students enroll in large courses together, as well as in a small integrative seminar. The cluster model is often the easiest form of learning community to implement because most of the curriculum does not change. What changes are the patterns of student enrollment, cohorts of students enrolled in larger classes, and in an additional seminar. The integrative seminar may be taught by experienced peers, by faculty, by academic advisors, by librarians, or by residence hall staff in the case of living/learning communities. The benefit for students, particularly first-term students, is that they become part of a social group that shares academic experiences, and they have an opportunity in the small seminar to practice integrating learning.

In *Radical Equations,* a Freshman Interest Group (FIG) offered at Western Washington University in 2003, a cohort of students enrolled in American history, college algebra, and a small seminar. Students in the seminar read selections from *Radical Equations: Civil Rights from Mississippi to the Algebra Project*, by Robert Moses and Charles Cobb, Jr. (2001), and discussed connections between history and mathematics. FIG students gave a presentation to the history course on the radical phase of the Civil Rights movement and according to the history instructor, the benefits of being part of the FIG were evident in the quality of students' presentations.[2]

Linked or clustered courses. In these learning communities, the students in both (or all three) courses are the same. Faculty teaching the courses plan integrative assignments, decide on shared or common readings, and develop other strategies to help students make both social and academic connections. Under the best circumstances, linked or clustered courses are scheduled so that they can be taught back-to-back, allowing flexibility for teachers and students, and faculty are supported in developing strategies for integrating content.

For instance, *Civil Rights: History and Criminal Justice* is a sixteen-week, six-credit learning community at Penn Valley Community College that links Introduction to Criminal Justice and American History. The learning community provides a historical and philosophical backdrop for the Civil Rights activities of the 1950s and 60s.[3] Taught by Greg Sanford and Karen Curls, the *Civil Rights* learning community examines U.S. laws within their historical context. The same group of students enrolls in both courses. At the end of the course, students and community members have the option to join their two faculty on a bus trip to Atlanta, Birmingham, Memphis, Montgomery, Selma, and Tuskegee to visit landmarks of the Civil Rights Movement.

Coordinated studies programs. Students enroll in a set of courses that have been fully integrated into a single program. Faculty and students do the work of the learning community as their full credit load, or as most of their load. Coordinated studies programs are typically designed so that students meet in a mix of small and large groups—including whole-program lectures, and smaller group meetings for seminars, workshops, and/or labs. The integrated nature of the program means that all the students and all faculty can be present together for extended periods of time. Some coordinated studies program last for more than one quarter, and the work students do in those programs reflects this.

The Folk: Power of an Image was a three-quarter interdisciplinary studies program created by Babacar M'Baye, Pat Krafcik, and Michael Pfeifer at The Evergreen State College, as a cross-cultural exploration of folk material—including tensions between the reality of folk life and the transforming of this reality into art, and the degree to which these transformations accurately convey the experience of folk culture or manipulate or distort it in Africa, Russia, and the United States.

The earliest documented experiment with learning communities in U.S. postsecondary education is Alexander Meikeljohn's Experimental College at the University of Wisconsin. Founded in 1927, the Experimental College was based in a residential college. The curriculum was organized as a single program rather than as a set of discrete courses, and the aim was to help students develop flexible thinking and good judgment. Faculty in the program were known as advisors, rather than as professors (Smith, MacGregor, et al. 2004).

The Experimental College lasted five years, but its key features—curriculum organized as a program rather than as discrete courses, purposeful connections between the curriculum and the co-curriculum, and student/faculty relationships focused on collaborative learning rather than on hierarchy and competition—are found in many learning communities today.

The intention behind the development of learning communities resonates with the much older tradition of indigenous education as described by Greg Cajete (1994). According to Cajete, indigenous education draws upon the rich contexts of spirituality, mythology, community, ecology, and art that are part of a holistic way of learning and knowing. Indigenous education aims to honor the whole person, and to remind learners that they are part of a rich and extensive social, historical, and natural world. Playing on the Latin root of education, *educare*, meaning to draw out, Cajete writes, "the goals of wholeness, self-knowledge, and wisdom are held in common by all the traditional educational philosophies around the world" (1994, 209). At heart, the learning community reform effort is rooted in similar goals. Most learning community faculty are, however, graduates of higher education in the United States, which is marked by its own history of exclusion and segregation based on race and ethnicity, and also income. Learning community faculty may aspire to values similar to the ones described by Cajete, but most have had educational experiences at odds with those values. As Paulo Freire (1998) points out, the conundrum educators find ourselves in is that at every moment, we are shaped by our histories—our particular genetic, socioeconomic, and historical circumstances—at the same time that we are actively engaged in a process of making history. The result is a perpetual play. In order to move immediately toward justice and educational equity, we must first acknowledge the impact of our individual and collective histories, how each has shaped how we think about the world. Then, we must consider how we can best work with others to change the path of those histories.

The Persistence of Inequities and the Implications for Educators

At a recent National Summer Institute on Learning Communities workshop, faculty, staff, and administrators were asked to describe the critical issues around diversity emerging on their campuses.[4] Among the observations shared by participants were the following:

> White faculty, staff, and students are turned off by any mention of diversity and there is lots of polarization around issues of

diversity, making it hard to move forward on anything. It's hard to get beyond the view that "I'm not prejudiced, I just have a problem with the way she presents herself" to a more systemic understanding of racism.

We often have a situation where there are one or two or three students of color in predominantly white classes.

When issues of bias and racism come up, students of color may not feel or actually be safe.

White students and campus employees are put off by what they perceive to be "self segregation" among students of color on campus.

On campuses with populations of immigrants and refugees, the needs of African students may be addressed while those of low-income African American students are ignored.

There is the widespread assumption that a campus is *not* diverse because people look alike.

Issues of lesbian, gay, bisexual, and transgender people are not being addressed, even in the presence of overt homophobia.

Students bring disparate skills to the classroom.

Students of color sometimes simply disappear from class.

The concerns raised by learning community practitioners in this workshop are similar to those voiced around the country. Many educators sense that conversations about diversity too often lead to more entrenched and polarized positions; the result: no action is taken on behalf of anyone. The emphasis in these conversations seems to shift quickly to feelings of anger, guilt, and defensiveness. We lose the chance to focus on an outcome that holds promise for reshaping the future. In Freire's terms, what is missing in many conversations, especially among whites, is an ability to account for history, for the socioeconomic forces that have been and are at play in shaping our present circumstances. As a result, conversations across significant differences—including race, socioeconomic class, nationality, and gender—are difficult and too infrequently arrive at a focus on justice.

Instead, campus conversations more often operate from a charity-based model, one that intends to create better circumstances within the limits of the status quo—without necessarily questioning what has enabled the very status quo that gives rise to the need for change. Many educators share an uneasy awareness that people's experiences differ in a number of ways—not just in terms of race, but also in terms of class, religion, gender, sexual orientation, disability, and nationality. Sometimes opportunities are created to give voice to some of those differences. While the impulse is good, the practice can go awry. On campuses where the majority of students are white, for instance, students of color are often asked to speak as if on behalf of a larger group, becoming in the process the "token" representative of an alternative perspective. This practice of inviting a member of a minority group to educate members of a majority group reinforces the dominance of the status quo—the minority perspective is typically offered as "enrichment" rather than as a contradiction requiring the rethinking of fundamental assumptions about the nature of our collective reality. At the same time, mindful of the limits of such practices, many faculty are working hard to figure out how to use the diverse experiences of students in their classes as a collective resource for learning. Educators have a growing awareness that the presence of diversity does not translate automatically into equity; many educators also realize that the hope of achieving equity lies in honoring and building upon the diverse perspective embodied by their students.

The challenge of translating diversity into equity has long been recognized, as has the powerful possibility of dialogue across real differences. In his now classic *The Souls of Black Folk*, W. E. B. Du Bois (1903) laments the lack of opportunity for social exchanges across racial lines. The consequences of the lack of opportunity for genuine exchange are described in that collection of essays, which lays out the staggering effects of grinding institutionalized racism on African American individuals, families, and communities. Du Bois believes that only through conversations between blacks and whites will whites, who hold all the political power, develop the insight and the collective will leading to the public policy decisions necessary to achieve racial equality. The repeal of the 1875 Civil Rights Act effectively halts the process of reconstruction, and Du Bois observes that as a result, "there is almost no community of intellectual life or point of transference where the thoughts and feelings of one race can come into direct contact and sympathy with the thoughts and feelings of others" (149). Consequently, he notes, "the very representatives of the two races who ought to be in complete understanding and sympathy for the welfare of the land and mutual benefit are so far strangers that one side thinks all whites are narrow and prejudiced and the other thinks educated

Negroes are dangerous and insolent" (149). When social conditions prohibit collaborative conversations across diverse perspectives, equity is not possible.

In an address to the National Association for the Advancement of Colored People (NAACP) in 1932, John Dewey, the educational reformer who helped shape the progressive education movement from which our contemporary learning community reform movement descends, argues a similar point: the problem facing ordinary people, especially people of color, is the lack of opportunity to discuss common problems and aspirations with others in similar circumstances. Instead, because of the economic, industrial, and financial systems, the interests of working people of all races are pitted against each other. What was needed—in 1932 and today—are opportunities for all repressed and oppressed minority groups to organize around their shared community of interest and to "discover remedies for the conditions that control (their collective) economic welfare" (1932, 228). With Du Bois, Dewey believed that the strategy for moving from diversity to equity lies in genuine exchange and collaboration across differences.

Dewey and Du Bois were both members of the Progressive Party, founded in 1912 by activists working for women's suffrage, racial equality, citizenship for Native Americans, tax reform, election reform, labor rights, conservation of natural resources, safe working conditions, and an end to child labor. As educators (Dewey at the University of Chicago and Columbia, Du Bois at Harvard, the University of Berlin, and Atlanta University) and activists, Dewey and Du Bois agreed on the critical role of education in helping develop citizens who would recognize how their individual interests were and are inexorably wrapped up in a larger collective practice. They lamented the lack of opportunity for exchange across significant differences aimed at shaping a common future. Noting that much of what is called selfishness is simply the outcome of limited observation coupled with limited imagination, Dewey argues that the primary purpose of education is to provide opportunities for "associated living," experiences in which an individual comes to understand how his/her actions affect others, and how the actions of others affect him/her (1927). Over time, Dewey writes, echoing Du Bois, the practice of conscious association will break down barriers based on race, class, and national origin, "widening the area of shared concerns, and (resulting in) the liberation of a greater diversity of personal capacities (1916, 87).

Dewey and Du Bois agree on the possibilities of education: through a genuine exchange across differences, people can come to recognize their common stake in a shared future, and develop strategies together for working toward a common good. The promise of this practice of education, however, is offset by the historical circumstances within the United States. As James Banks (2002) and others point out, educators in this country face the perpetual challenge of reconciling the ideals of inclusivity and democracy with a long history of institutionalized racism and inequality. The 1819 "Civilization Act," which aimed to assimilate Native Americans to dominant white culture; the 1830 Indian Removal Act; the 1831–38 Trail of Tears that forced resettlement of Indians to the west; the 1848 Treaty of Guadalupe Hidalgo that ceded Mexican territory in the southwest to the U.S. government; the 1882 ten-year prohibition of Chinese immigrants, which became an indefinite prohibition in 1902; the 1883 Supreme Court decision that struck down the Civil Rights Act of 1875 (the legal basis for Reconstruction after emancipation), claiming that the government could not regulate behavior of private individuals on matters of race relations; the 1896 *Plessy v. Ferguson* decision affirming the doctrine of "separate but equal"; and the 1942 Japanese American Internment Act, are all examples of institutionalized racism and inequality. The legacies of these decisions and others affect even those who have the opportunity to participate in postsecondary education in the United States, let alone those who participate in conversations aimed at addressing common issues.

To achieve educational equity, we need to notice the present patterns of participation and understand their history, analyze the factors that make it hard for these patterns to change, and then work collectively to make the necessary changes. This is an ambitious project, beyond the scope of the learning community reform movement alone. Income, race, and ethnicity have always influenced who participates in higher education, and these factors continue to affect patterns of participation in postsecondary education. The establishment of minority-serving institutions reflects the longstanding effort to address differential access to postsecondary education, including differential access to hospitable learning environments. Most of the 103 Historically Black Colleges and Universities (HBCU's) were founded in the late nineteenth century to serve African Americans who were legally prohibited from attending white higher education institutions in southern and border states. Even when states opened public HBCU's, the funding for them was always lower than that designated for white institutions: there was no pretense of equality (O'Brien and Zudak 1998). Most of the thirty-one tribal colleges established in the past thirty years by American Indian tribes provide affordable and culturally responsive education to tribal members. These tribal colleges have been developed as a marked alternative to predominantly white institutions, with their attendant history of pushing assimilation. About a fifth of all Native American students in postsecondary education in the United States are now enrolled in tribal colleges. The most recent development in minority serving intuitions are the designated Hispanic-Serving Institutions (HSI's), which currently number around 125. The HSI designation comes not from a particular intention to serve a particular population, but from having the equivalent of 25 percent full time equivalent Hispanic enrollment. HSI's are colleges and universities located in close geographic proximity to large Hispanic communities. Currently, about 42 percent of all Hispanic students are enrolled in HSI's. As such, HSI's reflect larger patterns of segregated housing across the United States (ibid).

Participation in higher education has always been tied to income. Since the 1970s, the PELL Grant and state initiatives have helped millions of lower- and middle-income students pursue postsecondary education, but this is changing. The GI Bill provided assistance for millions of veterans to attend universities, community colleges, and vocational schools after World War II and the Korean War. Today, however, the education and training benefits for American military personnel are much more modest than they were in the initial GI Bill. The combination of rising tuition, the declining value of individual PELL Grants, and state budget cuts have made higher education less affordable to veterans and non-veterans alike (American Political Science Association 2004). The 2005 federal spending bill will cause 90,000 low-income students to lose their PELL Grant eligibility, more than one million additional students face reductions in their PELL Grant awards, and the maximum Pell Grant is frozen at $4,050. At the same time, tuitions at four-year public institutions are 10.5 percent higher than they were in 2003.[5] Recent studies indicate that poor families spent 25 percent of their annual incomes in 2000 for education at a four-year college as compared with 13 percent in 1980, while middle-class families spent 7 percent in 2000 as compared with 4 percent in 1980. The wealthiest families continue to spend just 2 percent of their annual income on tuition (Rossides 2004). According to the National Center for Educational Statistics (NCES), 41 percent of African American students, 41 percent of American Indian students, and 38 percent of Hispanic students attending college come from families in the lowest income quartile, compared with 19 percent of white students who come from families in the lowest income quartile (1998).

As federal financial aid shrinks, differences in access to higher education are intensified. Although diversity does not lead to educational equity, the participation of diverse students in higher education is a necessary precursor to achieving equity. Maintaining the diversity of student enrollments achieved in the past few decades is critical (Rothstein 2004; Hurtado 1996), and keeping good state and federal financial aid programs is central to maintaining this diversity. So, too, is maintaining support for the community college systems across the country. Nearly half of the country's black and Hispanic students attend community colleges. Budget cuts to community college systems have significant effects on who enrolls in college. The Los Angeles Community College District, for instance, estimated that it would turn away about 6,000 Hispanic students in fall 2003—more than five times the number of Hispanic freshmen admitted to the University of California at Los Angeles in 2002–03 (Evelyn 2003). A Century Foundation study found that in the absence of affirmative action policies, if the 146 most selective colleges in the country used *only* grades and test scores as admissions criteria, about 5,000 fewer black and Hispanic students would be admitted each year. In contrast, officials estimated that at least 20,000 black and Hispanic students would be shut out of California's community college system alone in 2003–04 because of cuts in state spending (ibid).

Access to postsecondary education has always been influenced by race and by income; it is also influenced by ethnicity. Underdeveloped educational policies on linguistic diversity present a barrier to many people in the United States. As Juan Gonzalez points out in *Harvest of Empire: A History of Latinos in America* (2000), unlike many other nations, the United States has yet to recognize the right of language minorities to protection against discrimination (272). In particular, the tendency towards an English Only policy exacerbates historical conflicts with Spanish-speaking people who were involuntarily made citizens of the English-speaking United States. While many argue that learning English is necessary to function in the world of work and even to act in the capacity of citizen, the question of how best to achieve this goal remains under debate. Given the growing number of people who speak languages other than English at home, we need more classes intended to help non-native speakers learn English at all levels. Educators estimate, however, that although approximately 14 million residents born outside the United States would benefit from ESL classes, federal funds pay for only 10 percent—between 1.4 million and 1.5 million ESL slots each year.

The educational achievement gap between students of color and white students at all levels of education continues to grow.[6] In terms of college graduation, minority students are less equal now than they were thirty years ago (Bensimon 2004; Rothstein 2004; Bok 2003). Martha Lamkin (2004) lists the following sobering facts in a recent Lumina Foundation report:

a) Although 59 percent of white students earn a bachelor's degree within six years of entering college, the same is true of only 39 percent of African American students and only 37 percent of Latino students.
b) Only 7 percent of young people from the lowest-income families earn four-year degrees by age twenty-six; among young people from high-income families, the number is 60 percent.
c) At four-year colleges, 26 percent of freshmen drop out before their sophomore year; at two-year institutions, the first-year attrition rate is 45 percent.

At the same time that substantially increasing participation and completion rates for students of color and low-income students appear to be beyond our collective grasp, the benefits of earning a college degree are increasingly clear. On average, college graduates earn 70 percent more than high school graduates, and high school dropouts are four times more likely than college graduates to be unemployed. Only 29 percent of all Americans in their mid- to late-twenties have completed B.A. degrees, and 7 percent have A.A. degrees. Only 18 percent of African Americans and 9 percent of Hispanics between twenty-five and twenty-nine have earned a B.A. (Kazis, Vargas, and Hoffman 2004).

The promise of learning communities is that they can help people develop the skills and abilities needed to address these inequities. At the beginning of the twentieth century, both Du Bois and Dewey argued that the purpose of education is to create conditions for genuine exchange across significant differences leading to strategies for acting collectively to address shared public issues. A necessary condition for these conversations, then and now, is the very presence of people from diverse backgrounds participating in these conversations. The history of our country, including the legacies of segregation, racism, and privilege, affects our present collective circumstances in a way that makes these conversations difficult. Building as it does upon successful completion of years of schooling, access to postsecondary education is already restricted based on class, race, and ethnicity. In this context, the promise held out by intentionally creating communities of learners on our college campuses is high; at the same time, the challenges we face in making sure that this reform effort contributes to educational equity, rather than becoming a strategy that underscores the current patterns of inclusion and exclusion, are equally great.

Participants in the workshop at the National Summer Institute on Learning Communities discussed the complexity of creating learning communities that support all learners. They recognized that the architecture of a learning community does not in itself guarantee the outcome of educational equity for the students participating in it. They also were conscious that the focus within learning community programs and even within the administration of such programs is frequently not on the larger social context that gives rise to equity issues. Although learning communities on many campuses are fostering educational equity in a variety of ways, the question before us is still, as Patrick Hill (n.d.) writes, how we encourage citizens to sustain conversations of respect with diverse others for the sake of making public policy together, forging over and over again a shared future. As a reform effort, learning communities are situated broadly within the tradition of progressive education in the United States, specifically within the context of local, national, and global issues requiring our best, more rigorous, and multifaceted thinking. The extent to which learning communities will help educate citizens who are able to contribute collaboratively to addressing those issues, working for equity within and beyond our campuses, remains to be seen. Adopting two strategies from longstanding work on equity issues increases the likelihood that learning communities will contribute to educational equity.

Institutional Data and the Location of Learning Communities

One of the most promising projects aimed at achieving equity is the analytical, action research approach developed by Estela Mara Bensimon and her colleagues at the Center for Urban Education at the University of Southern California. They have developed the Diversity Scorecard project as a model of research-as-praxis to advance equity in educational outcomes. The project is based on two key assumptions. First, within most colleges and universities in the United States, whether the campuses are highly selective and predominantly white, open access and relatively heterogeneous, or classified as Hispanic-serving, academic achievement is stratified based on race. This means that the presence of diverse students on a campus does not guarantee that all students are equally well served by the institution: diversity and educational equity are not synonymous. Second, in order to create change within an institution, individuals who work at that institution must see for themselves the magnitude of the inequities, analyze and internalize the meaning of these inequities, and ultimately be moved to act upon them. In the Diversity Scorecard project, campus teams are invited to gather data related to four dimensions of institutional performance with respect to equity in outcomes: access, retention, institutional receptivity, and excellence. The aim of the project is for campus team members to develop a deep understanding of educational inequities by creating the tools leading to their own recognition of the problem and a subsequent commitment to address it (Bensimon 2004).[7]

A parallel project—analytical, data-driven, and team-based—evolved in Washington State as a collaborative effort by multicultural affairs directors in community and technical colleges, institutional researchers, deans of instruction, and staff from both the State Board for Community and Technical Colleges and the Washington Center for Improving the Quality of Undergraduate Education. This statewide working group developed a framework that helps campus teams use existing institutional data to look at eight dimensions of their institution: access, student progression, student goal attainment and completion, hiring and retaining of diverse faculty and staff, instruction, student support services, institutional and administrative policies, and physical environment. The premise of the Framework for Diversity Assessment and Planning project is similar to that of the Diversity Scorecard: campus teams working together to gather and interpret data related to educational equity for students of color can become a powerful force for institutional change.[8]

With increasing frequency, campuses are intentionally situating learning communities at critical entry or transition points to support the academic achievement and sense of belonging of students of color and first-generation students. Federally funded Title V programs (serving Hispanic students) and Title III programs (serving first-generation and low-income students) often use learning communities as a core strategy (Smith, MacGregor, et al. 2004). Of the Title V programs funded in 2002, for instance, approximately one third explicitly named learning communities as a strategy for improving the retention and academic achievement of Hispanic students.[9] The University of Texas at El Paso (UTEP), a Hispanic majority (73 percent in fall 2003) research-intensive university, used funds from the National

Science Foundation to develop learning communities to support students intent upon majoring in engineering or science (Lardner 2004). More recently, with support from Title V funds, UTEP has developed a range of learning community models aimed at helping students form social and academic communities, strengthen their academic performance, make connections across disciplines, and develop a sense of belonging on campus (Smith, Ward, et al. 2004). The purpose of the learning communities that are part of these federal grants is to boost retention and achievement rates by creating cohorts of students supported by members of the academic communities they intend to join.

In *The Pedagogy of Possibilities: Developmental Education, College-Level Studies, and Learning Communities*, Gillies Malnarich (2003) argues that learning communities can effectively be used as deliberate intervention strategies to address trouble spots in the curriculum, including:

- high risk courses where 30 percent of students drift away after one month;
- graveyard courses where 50 percent of students earn low grades or drop out;
- gateway courses that have a reputation among students for being tough;
- platform courses for entry into professional and technical programs; and
- transition courses for developmental and second-language speakers moving into liberal arts and professional/technical programs. (44)

Malnarich argues that we should focus on the places where we have created a curriculum that is "risky"—rather than labeling students as being "at risk." She urges educators to notice where the curriculum puts students at risk and to move quickly to change those curricular trouble spots. Malnarich further argues that a core strategy for connecting learning communities with the aim of educational equity is to site them in these critical places, using data from the institution. Recognizing places where the curriculum puts students at risk is a fundamental obligation of educators committed to equity. As Malnarich points out, those students who finally do arrive in higher education—particularly low-income and first-generation students, and students of color—are heroic; we can't afford to lose any of them. *The Pedagogy of Possibilities* describes over a dozen learning community programs that effectively combine high expectations, intellectual rigor, and academic and social support for students who are considered to be academically under-prepared.

Campus teams participating in the National Summer Institute on Learning Communities held annually at The Evergreen State College are now asked to prepare campus fact sheets prior to the institute. These fact sheets are designed to help teams analyze patterns of student enrollment and success, and decide, based on this data, on the most strategic places for learning communities to be sited, given the aim of reaching educational equity. The fact sheet helps teams surface potential tensions between where faculty would like to create learning communities—between pairs of very congenial colleagues, for instance, deeply interested in each other's upper-division course material—and courses in which large numbers of students appear to stall out, for instance in large introductory courses, or required courses in math or writing. The fact sheet does not dictate what teams will decide to do, but it does help teams make decisions about developing learning communities that are informed by larger issues of student success.

The Evergreen State College-Tacoma program is a nationally recognized example of a learning community designed expressly to support the learning of working adults in the Hilltop neighborhood of Tacoma, Washington, the majority of whom are African American (see Joye Hardiman's description of the program in Lardner 2004). Faculty work collaboratively to develop a thematic focus for the year that connects students' lives and community issues, giving rise to a curriculum grounded in genuine questions that matter in the world. The program is designed around the core values of hospitality, reciprocity, inclusivity, and civility and these values are manifest in the curriculum and the pedagogy of the program, as well as in the physical design of the campus space and the scheduling of classes. It takes the form of a cluster of team-taught courses linked by an overarching theme as well as a weekly Lyceum—an integrative seminar. Courses are offered from 10 a.m. to 1 p.m., and then again from 6 p.m. to 9 p.m., which means students who have to miss class during their regularly scheduled time have an opportunity to make it up during the other time block. The nature of the program theme varies each year, but it always connects community issues and students lives' within the curriculum. For instance, when the program theme focused on urban studies and institutional dynamics, microbiologist Willie Parson team-taught a course with attorney Barbara Laners on urban public policy.

Laners and Parson and their students analyzed federal, state, and local public policy making, particularly its impact on urban communities. In winter, Parson teamed with Gilda Sheppard, a sociologist, in a class that used scientific and sociological perspectives to examine media representations of public health issues, particularly HIV-AIDS. Students developed an array of educational materials for audiences ranging from children to senior citizens. In spring quarter, Parson teamed with environmental scientist Tyrus Smith and developed a course where students used environmental and physiological studies of the Tacoma waterfront as the basis for their statistical analyses (Parson 2002). The Evergreen -Tacoma program provides an exemplary model of a learning community program grounded in a commitment to equity and to educating citizens who will be able to address public issues together, as the high retention and graduation rates, along with the accomplishments of Tacoma graduates, demonstrate.

The Positionality of Our Experiences and Perspectives

The recognition that our thinking is shaped by our lived experiences has been widely discussed across disciplines. The central assumption behind this view of situated knowledge is that all knowledge, all theories, are generated from the standpoint of particular interests, locations, and life experiences (Bensimon 1994; Harding 1991). Edgar Beckham (2004) refers to this as *positionality*—the synthesis of where each of us "is at" and where each of us is "coming from," students, faculty, staff, and college presidents alike. Recognizing positionality, the "situated-ness" of my knowing, depends on my ability to appreciate that how I understand the world has been shaped by my particular historical, economic, and sociological circumstances. Understanding the situatedness of my own perspective means learning to appreciate how factors beyond my control, including my race, class, ethnicity, gender, religion, sexual orientation, disabilities or abilities, nationality, and language spoken at home affect me, the way others perceive me, and the circumstances I find myself in.[10] In terms of work on diversity and equity, recognizing positionality is fundamental; everything else builds upon that, including an analysis of systems of privilege and power based on social identities. Patrick Hill (n.d.) argues that a central goal of learning communities should be to invite students (and of necessity, faculty) to become aware of the partiality and limitations of our experience, to develop the confidence and skills to share that experience—partial as it is—and move toward a less partial understanding of the world, of others, and of ourselves by developing skills and dispositions so that we can learn with and from others.

Inviting students to recognize the partiality of their own views, to develop a certain level of epistemological humility based on the awareness of the limits of any one person's view including their own, is crucial. Drawing on her work with pre-service teachers, Sonia Nieto (1999) writes that the inability to recognize the limits of our own perceptions is a fundamental problem facing schools: many contemporary white educators identify as being "just an American"—absent any ethnicity, absent a connection with history. The problem with this "just an American" view is that it erases history, reinforcing a view of the United States as a straightforward meritocracy, a country where the material conditions in people's lives can be accounted for simply in terms of their persistence and good luck.[11] The social stratification that gives rise to the need to recognize differences in privilege, power, and perspective also limits opportunities for exchanges across perspectives in the first place.

A student in a summer class wrote a dialogue that illustrates how conversations between students are shaped by the situatedness of their perspectives and the ways in which, as Edgar Beckham (2004) writes, the social history of the United States erupts into the present. The assignment called for developing a text based on two voices.[12] Another student in the class—a white student—was writing about breaking up with the man she had married at age seventeen. An older white student returning to college nearly twenty years after graduating from high school was writing about the different ways she and her neighbor started their gardens. The student whose essay is excerpted here is a young African American woman just starting college. In this dialogue, she is trying to imagine how two young people can have a substantive conversation about race and racism across their significantly different ways of understanding the world.

> Two average people narrate this essay.
> One is black; the other is white.
>
> BP: "Your people enslaved us and have yet to apologize or give any kind of reparation."
>
> WP: "I didn't enslave your people; how can you hold me responsible for something I didn't do?"
>
> BP: "For my people slavery is a generational curse that won't go away and your people brought the curse on us.

> Why won't you stand up and take responsibility for what your people did? Don't you have some pride in yourself? You're too quick to shake off your connections to your ancestors; where is your pride?"
>
> WP: "Wouldn't you be quick to shake off something so shameful? I know my ancestors did a lot of things wrong. . . .What happened to your ancestors and what's happening to you today is wrong, but there's nothing I can do about that. The damage is already done. The hurt and pain of your people is too deep. Tell me, what can be done?"

This student's dialogue captures the complexity of the dynamics that inform conversations and interactions in the classroom all the time. In her dialogue, she makes explicit how social history and our different relationships with that history shape even a brief conversation in the present. Without an appreciation of our shared history, and without deep reflection particularly for whites about that history, a conversation that begins this way—"your people enslaved us"—can quickly go awry, cementing polarized positions and reinforcing frustration on all sides.

Given that most faculty and administrators in higher education generally, and learning communities in particular, are white, understanding the nature of whiteness and white privilege is a critical foundation. Peggy McIntosh's (1988) groundbreaking work on white privilege is an extremely useful and accessible place to begin. McIntosh argues that white privilege is at once pervasive *and* taboo because the acknowledgment of white privilege flies in the face of the American myth of a meritocracy. Describing her development as a white woman in the United States, McIntosh writes that in no way did her schooling prepare her to see herself as unfairly advantaged, or as an oppressor; instead, she was taught to see herself as an individual shaped by her individual moral will. McIntosh argues that whites need to do more consistent work to understand how unearned race advantage and the dominance that goes with it actually affect our daily lives. Many white people in the United States—students and faculty—do not see "whiteness" as a racial identity, and do not see racism as a problem affecting them because they are not people of color.[13] Race is a critical social identity to investigate, but race is not the only advantaging system at work. McIntosh argues that we need to work as well on examining the daily experience of having gender advantage, or ethnic advantage, or physical ability, or advantage related to nationality, religion, or sexual orientation (ibid).

Given the role of the United States in the world, for U.S. citizens, nationality has become another social identity requiring critical investigation for the ways in which it—in conjunction with an individual's other social identities—shapes perceptions. Those of us who are U.S. citizens have to recognize the limits of our national perspective with as much alacrity as we are learning to recognize the blind spots arising from our other social identities. As Grant Cornwell and Eve Stoddard argue, "in the process of becoming more self-aware, students need to develop the capacity to discern their social locations in every relation, transaction, and encounter. Just as race studies in the United States have led to critical white studies and the realization that the dominant group needs scrutiny, so in the global context, U.S. students need to learn about their power and privilege in relation to most of the world's population" (1999, 24). In his 1982 Nobel Prize acceptance speech, Gabriel García Márquez eloquently argues for the epistemological humility that comes from scrutinizing positionality, including nationality, and leads those of us in the most developed and powerful countries to realize the distortions that come from imposing one's own patterns for interpreting reality on the lives of people in other countries: "The interpretation of our reality (in Latin America) through patterns not our own serves only to make us more unknown, ever less free, ever more solitary." From the most global level—nation to nation—to the most personal level—one to another—a core ability in the formation of genuine learning communities is the ability to recognize our own patterns for interpreting reality, to resist applying our patterns to others, and to be open to and interested in learning about the patterns used by others.

Scrutinizing our own positions as educators is a prerequisite for creating welcoming and inclusive classrooms. Students sense in the first few moments of an interaction whether or not they will be welcome in a particular setting, and when students feel they are in a caring and supportive environment, one that is respectful of their social identities, they learn (Zull 2002; Nieto 1999; Steele 1992). Creating a welcoming environment for all students is critical if we are going to move towards equity in education, particularly on heterogeneous campuses. The benefits of working with diverse peers have been clearly documented (Hurtado, et al. 1999). Increasing ethnic/racial diversity, however, without attending to issues of campus climate, particularly the racial climate, often results in difficulties for students of color as well as for white students. Sylvia Hurtado's (1996) research suggests that the presence of small populations of historically under-represented groups on predominantly white campuses tends to create conditions where students of color are perceived as tokens, rather than as individuals. As a result, minority students are frequently left feeling alienated due to what are perceived as inhospitable practices.

From the perspective of educational research, experiencing a sense of belonging is crucial for academic success. Ernest Pascarella and Patrick Terenzini (1991) argue that students who have a high sense of belonging and are very involved with peers, faculty, and institutional activities are likely to be academically successful. For first-generation learners and students of color, though, negotiating this sense of belonging is complex. As William Tierney (1992) points out, until recently U.S. colleges and universities were designed to educate a clientele composed primarily of white, middle- and upper-class males. Research on student involvement has tended to put the responsibility for making a place for themselves on the students. As a result, students often have different perceptions of how welcoming a campus is. For instance, Chalsa Loo and Garry Rolison (1986) found that at one institution, 68 percent of white students and only 28 percent of African American and Chicano students thought the university was generally supportive of minority students. In response to these differences, Laura Rendón (2004) argues that colleges need to adopt a very proactive approach to making students feel welcome, which she terms *validation*. Validation is an enabling, confirming, and supportive process initiated by people in the college or university, in or out of class, that shifts the focus from what students need to do to what members of the university can do. In other words, faculty, staff, and administrators are expected to take the first steps in reaching out to students, helping them believe in themselves and their inherent capacities to learn (Rendón, García, and Person 2004).

The learning community program at the University of New Mexico, *Freshman Academic Choices*, has been explicitly designed to validate students. The fundamental pedagogical approach of the FAC program can best be described in terms of Robert Ibarra's (2001) conceptual framework, multicontextuality. The central assumption in Ibarra's framework is that the cultural frameworks within which individuals develop influence how we learn and express ourselves. Multicontextuality is based in part on a polarity between high and low context, where low-context is associated with traditional university values—objectivity, abstraction, non-contextualized information—and high context is associated with community, collaboration, and contextualized knowledge built through an interactive process. As Joel

Nossoff and Dan Young (2004) write, "the interdisciplinary, community-oriented, collaborative approaches of our *Freshman Academic Choices* address the strengths of our high-context students and help them in their transition to understanding and being able to succeed within the low-context world of academia. Our low-context students gain as well by—among other things—benefiting from the increased opportunities to actively process and reflect on their learning while also making sense of diverse perspectives" (19). The process of validating students is based on an awareness of students as whole people, and as is the case in the FAC program, it leads to a practice of inclusive pedagogy grounded in an awareness of positionality, focused on students as personal, political, and intellectual beings (Howell and Tuitt 2003).

Characteristics of Effective Learning Communities

In addition to being situated in places that can make a difference for students—for instance, in curricular trouble spots—as well as reflecting a deep investigation of the positionality of perspectives, effective learning communities share a set of defining characteristics. Educators "infuse intellectually rigorous, inclusive curriculum with high expectations; (they) design developmentally appropriate assignments and award fluid credits" based on the work students are able to do; and they "invite students to participate in the creation of knowledge" (Malnarich 2005, 59–60).

Intellectually rigorous and inclusive curriculum

Intellectual rigor and high expectations take several forms. Many learning communities assign trade books and primary source material, rather than text books, so that students have more opportunities to study ideas in depth, and to develop a sense of intellectual history and scope. Moreover, the questions and problems that lie at the heart of the learning community are similar to those faced by groups of people in the world: the relationship between what we invite students to do inside school and what we hope they will be able to do outside school is clear. In learning communities involving developmental studies courses, students learn to do college-level work by actually doing it, with support from their developmental courses (Malnarich 2005).

In addition to being rigorous, the curriculum of effective learning communities needs to be inclusive. Given our aspirations to create welcoming learning environments and to achieve educational equity, developing curricular materials that acknowledge, value, and reflect multiple points of view and ways of knowing the world is critical. As Martha Nussbaum (1997) points out, however, the exclusion of groups of people from higher education—women, African Americans, other ethnic minorities—also meant excluding the lives of these people from the official domains of knowledge. Nussbaum points out that these exclusions are invisible, appearing simply as the tradition we inherit. Consequently, she writes, because the exclusions seem natural, they also appear to be apolitical—only the demand for inclusion is interpreted as being "politically motivated" (7).

The effort to develop more inclusive curricula in the United States is not new. Formal efforts to develop a more inclusive curriculum in higher education have their early roots in efforts to reduce intergroup prejudice and related human relations work beginning in the 1940s and 50s, based on the assumption that awareness of differences in perspective would reduce prejudice. In the 1950s, cross-cultural and international training programs were designed to prepare students to study in other countries. Black and ethnic studies emerged from the civil rights movement in the 1960s, rooted in a critique of what was being taught in the universities—what, by whom, and for whom. The 1970s gave birth to the women's movement and consciousness-raising as a strategy for critical self-reflection, connecting personal stories to larger social realities. (Adams, Bell, and Griffin 1997). Currently, many campuses have instituted diversity requirements as part of their degree requirements. A National Panel convened by the American Association of Colleges and Universities (AACU) recommends that campus diversity requirements encourage students to explore four dimensions of U.S. diversity, including the student's own inherited and constructed traditions and identity; the history of diverse groups within the United States in terms of their experience of democracy and the pursuit of equality; hands-on experiences with community-based efforts to redress systemic social inequities; and practice with sustained forms of inquiry into contested issues.[14] These National Panel recommendations bridge early efforts to expand the curriculum by adding "supplementary" materials to more recent efforts to transform it, changing the core assumptions about what counts as "knowledge."[15]

Estela Mara Bensimon (1994) usefully distinguishes among approaches to curriculum transformation, ranging from those she describes as taking an additive approach to those she describes as emerging from a "paradigmatic shift" in the way that both knowledge and pedagogy are conceptualized. A paradigmatic shift depends upon teachers' willingness to reconceptualize the traditional hierarchical relationship between teachers and students and to rethink the notion that there is a single body of intellectual knowledge (61).

One of the most striking examples of a culturally responsive learning community program in which both curriculum and pedagogy have been transformed is the *Power and Limits of Dialogue* program (PALOD) at The Evergreen State College. Developed by Patrick Hill and Angela Gilliam, PALOD has been offered as both a full-time and a half-time team-taught interdisciplinary learning community program that runs for two quarters. Credits are awarded in philosophy, anthropology, sociology, political economy, and the theory and practice of interpersonal communication. The first quarter of the program emphasizes models of human differences and varieties of dialogues and dialogical skills, strategies, and expectations. Dialogues with environmentalists and loggers, Palestinians and Israelis, and African Americans and whites are introduced. The second quarter focuses on two or three dialogues, emphasizing interracial issues, particularly reconciliation and reparation in a global context. In both quarters, particular dialogues are approached as case studies for understanding the power and limitations of dialogue. In describing the program for prospective students, Hill and Gilliam write, "each student will sense over the course of the program that he/she can internalize the dialogical skills as add-ons to already existing strategies of survival; and/or as the adoption of fundamentally depolarizing habits of mind and heart now widely seen as vital to a pluralistic age in need of a more functional understanding of our differences. This program might in part be described as a six-month experiment in understanding, in unprecedented, radical or respectful listening."[16]

The practice of radical listening, rather than a more defined product, figures prominently in PALOD students' final portfolios. Students keep a log of the hours they spend on project work, recording the blocks of time they invest in making dialogue possible even if the dialogue never happens. Success is measured in terms of students' willingness to create conditions where dialogue can happen; they are not held responsible for making sure that a dialogue does happen. The final written assignment takes the form of an integrative exam, which Hill and Gilliam characterize as being closer to a lengthy journal entry or a goodbye letter to classmates than to a traditional exam. It is explicitly designed to help students synthesize and make public their learning in a way that is useful for their peers. Consistent with Bensimon's description of a paradigmatic change, the PALOD learning community program embodies transformed relationships between faculty and students and among students so that students in the program can focus on how and what they are learning, in a rigorous and inclusive way.

Developmentally-appropriate assignments
Effective learning communities are characterized by assignments based on genuine questions or issues, which allow for a range of responses. In some learning community programs involving English courses, for instance, students are evaluated based on a final portfolio. Depending on the quality of work in the portfolio, students may earn credit for college-level English or for developmental English. The focus of their learning is the same, however. Imagine another example: a mix of pre-service and practicing teachers enroll in an intensive summer course on the teaching of writing with a focus on grammar, and they are discussing the introduction to a collection of essays entitled *Language Diversity in the Classroom*, edited by Geneva Smitherman and Victor Villanueva (2003). One young woman has just asked why, if dialects are just as complex and rule-based as Standard English, teachers have to prepare students to use Standard English almost exclusively. An experienced middle-school teacher, keeping her impatience in check, replies: "It's fine to want to change the world. Kids need to know how to speak and write in ways that match the status quo. Call it the language of power if you like. But if you can't write with correct grammar, no one will take you seriously." Another teacher enters into the conversation, assuring her colleagues that the solution is simple: honor your students' home languages, *and* teach them to use standard written English. Then, this student remembers growing up in the South and having her accent "coached" out of her so that she will sound "smart." Another woman who grew up in rural Panama without access to secondary schooling talks about her experience emigrating to the United States, enrolling in English classes, and then dropping out for several years because she felt so inept. She preferred learning English outside of school, where she felt herself to be smart.

Most of the participants in the class grew up speaking English at home, and their formal schooling had been in English. While they had some concerns about their own grammar, they had not, for the most part, developed a critical awareness around the teaching of standard written English in school. Through the course readings and more important, through conversations with each other, they gradually came to see that they too had questions about a central concern in the field of English studies: how best to support students as they learn to negotiate the particular standards and conventions that are part of academic writing. The portfolios created by students in this seminar varied in their intellectual sophistication and in their clarity, and students' evaluations reflected those differences. In spite of significant differences in skills and backgrounds, all the seminar participants, like David Bartholomae (1988) and Mina Shaughnessey (1977) before them, turned their attention to a major "trouble spot" in the curriculum: the varieties of English spoken, the complex nature of academic discourse, and the multiple demands students face as they learn to make a place for themselves within that discourse.

Curricular changes necessitate changes in pedagogy, as the seminar participants discovered. The key to making learning inclusive is to design strategies that build on and honor the perspectives and experiences that each student brings. Then, educators need to take explicit steps to help students learn from each other as well. Learning always builds on what we already know, and developmentally appropriate assignments help students connect what they know with what they are learning, supporting without limiting intellectual development. In *Pedagogy of Freedom* (1998), Paulo Freire argues that his role as a teacher of mathematics or biology (or any other subject) is not simply teaching subject matter, but rather helping students recognize that they are "the architects of their own cognition process" (112). For Freire, the key to this transformative approach is twofold: the teacher is always also a learner, and secondly, the invitation extended to students, regardless of the discipline, is to recognize that they are simultaneously shaped by all they have learned, and that they are the creators of their own learning. Lee Shulman (2004) argues that to take learning seriously, we have to take learners seriously and we have to help learners discover what it is they already know. New learning comes from applying old understandings to new ideas and experiences, and new learning is enriched immensely through social interactions with other learners who are also wrestling with connecting old understandings and new ideas. Shulman writes that what lies at the heart of powerful learning are opportunities for "active, collaborative, reflective reexamination of ideas in a social context" (36). Developmentally appropriate assignments in the context of learning communities create exactly these kinds of opportunities.

Students construct knowledge together

A theme throughout Dewey's writing is the precarious balance between our evolving ability to work on problems together for the sake of our common future, and the rapid pace of industrial and technological change that seems to put the most critical issues well beyond the scope of ordinary citizens. In "American Education Past and Future," Dewey writes, "the sense of unsolved social problems is all about us. There are problems of crime, of regard for law, of capital, of labor, of unemployment, of stability and security, of family life, of war and peace, of international relations and cooperation—all on a larger scale than the world has ever seen before. . . . Unless education prepares future citizens to deal effectively with these great questions, our civilization may collapse" (1931, 94). He argues that we are engaged in a contest between "mis-education," which bears no relation to the needs and conditions of the modern world, and a possible education, which helps us face the future more effectively and collaboratively.

Writing fifty years later, John Kemeny, president of Dartmouth and chairman of President Carter's commission investigating the causes of the disaster at Three-Mile Island, makes a similar argument about the right purpose of education given the kinds of citizens we need: "[We] desperately need individuals who can pull together knowledge from a wide variety of fields and integrate it in one mind. We are in an age when we are facing problems that no one discipline can solve. . . . What we'd like our best students to be able to do is to walk in on a problem they know nothing at all about and by working hard in six months become fairly expert on it."[17] David Rossides (2004) makes much the same case when he argues that the center of gravity in a curriculum ought to be the most pressing problems a society faces.

The *Local Knowledge* program, a yearlong learning community program taught by Lin Nelson and Ann Fischel at The Evergreen State College, was designed to help students develop the skills to sort through perplexing issues, connecting local, national, and international issues. As Fischel and Nelson (2002) write, students in the program were expected to take themselves seriously as citizen-learners. Students worked in teams with community-based mentors from a range of local organizations including the Cold and Hungry Coalition, Garden Raised Bounty, Mason County Literacy, and Public Employees for Environmental Responsibility. Drawing on media studies and environmental studies, the focus of the program was on "how people experience and define themselves in community, how they value (or de-value) their lives and the lives of their neighbors, how they interpret and analyze their reality, and how they come to do politically engaged work—from challenging local authorities over official treatment of the homeless to creating public space to discuss the war in Afghanistan" (32). The program included seminars, field trips, meetings with community mentors, workshops on survey design, video production, interviewing, and research—library, archival, and community-based—plus panels on community fundraising, alternative economic development, local media, and nongovernmental organizations. At the end of the year, community mentors reported that students made genuine contributions to their projects. In their self-evaluations, students described their own rich learning, including the ability to use knowledge gained in school to help address larger public issues.

Educating for Compassion

The simultaneous recognition that our future is shared while our thinking is grounded in our particular experiences of the world underscores the need to learn together in communities. Learning community structures create educational opportunities for developing the habits of mind necessary to participate effectively and collaboratively in a pluralistic and democratic society. Given the structured opportunities for social and integrated learning, learning communities become rich sites for addressing complex problems that defy the boundaries of any single discipline. Learning communities can become places where students and teachers experience the gift of learning with others who understand the world differently not just because of disciplinary differences, but also because of genuine differences in how we experience and interpret reality, how and where we are situated, and the social identities that shape our thinking. What animates an effective learning community is a sense of our shared future, a mindfulness about our responsibility to imagine a larger public good to which we can work.

One way to understand this animating principle for learning communities is in terms of compassion—a series of judgments that lead us to be moved to act on behalf of others. According to Nussbaum (2003), compassion is not a feeling; rather, it consists of a series of decisions or judgments of which we can become more conscious. The first step in compassion is making a decision about the seriousness of the situation that others find themselves in, a decision limited only by our ability to imagine those circumstances. The next step is deciding that the situation is undeserved—it has simply happened to people. Then, we decide that a similar thing could happen to us: were we in a different location, we too could become victims of war or famine or mudslides. We too could be facing the consequences of massive lay-offs or environmental hazards. Finally, compassion requires that we decide to include more people, including distant others, within the circle of people we care about and are moved to act on behalf of (ibid). Ultimately, our ability to make public policy together—locally, nationally, globally—depends upon how deeply we have learned to practice compassion.

This description of compassion as a decision-making process shows how things can go wrong. We may not be able to imagine the suffering of others. For instance, hearing statistics about incarceration rates doesn't automatically translate into an appreciation of what that means for families and communities, just as learning about U.S. foreign policies doesn't translate automatically into an appreciation of the effects of those policies on other people's lives. On campuses, white students often underestimate the effects of racism on students of color. Men may underestimate the effects of sexism on women. A critical task for educators in learning communities is to help students use their imaginative and empathetic capacities to appreciate the circumstances that other people find themselves in.

Other judgments can go wrong as well. A classic error is that of "blaming the victim" rather than analyzing structural inequalities and the circumstances beyond someone's control. The comment, "I'm not racist, I just have a problem with the way she presents herself" is an example of this faulty thinking. People who have lived relatively privileged lives often cannot imagine the material circumstances of other people's lives. The inability to imagine living in profoundly different circumstances can lead to an inability or an unwillingness to recognize that the suffering of others is caused by social injustices or inequities. Instead, we make a judgment that somehow other people are responsible for the circumstances they find themselves in.

Another danger of uneducated compassion is that we can move too easily from having compassion only for our own children, our own families, the people we know best—to wanting to promote the well-being of "our" people *over* all other people. Nussbaum cites the aftermath of 9/11 as an example of overvaluing some lives relative to others. She writes, "we think the events of September 11 are bad because they involved *us* and *our* nation. Not just human lives, but *American* lives. The world came to a stop—in a way that it rarely has for Americans when disaster has befallen human beings in other places. . . . Floods, earthquakes, cyclones, the daily deaths of thousands from preventable malnutrition and disease—none of these makes the American world come to a standstill, none elicits a tremendous outpouring of grief and compassion" (2003, 13).

Effective learning communities offer opportunities for teachers and students alike to learn to imagine the realities of each others' lives, as well as the lives of people beyond the walls of the academy. As Carolyn Vasques-Scalera notes, "all students and faculty bring a wealth of tradition, information, and experience to their understandings of the world, and that wealth can contribute in meaningful ways to the learning process" (2002). Achieving educational equity depends on our ability to understand the genuine differences in people's lived experiences, to appreciate that these differences are not wholly of anyone's making but are also a legacy of segregation and exclusion, and to act together to create a better future.

Endnotes

1. In 2003, one third of all first-year students responding to the survey indicated that they had already participated in or planned to participate in a learning community. To view the NSSE 2004 Annual report, see http://www.indiana.edu/~nsse/html/report-2004.shtml.
2. See "A Radical Idea—Or, How a Civil Rights Leader Inspired an Interdisciplinary Approach to Learning Quantitative Concepts in Real-World Contexts" by Karen Casto in the Fall 2003 issue of the *Washington Center News* for more information.
3. From "Civil Rights Learning Community: An Overview" presented by Karen Curls and Greg Sanford at the Midwest learning community conference, November 2004. For more information on this learning community, see http://news.pennvalleycc.com.
4. June 22, 2003 at The Evergreen State College.
5. Source: www.uspirg.org.
6. Academic achievement depends on a number of well-documented factors, including access to food, medical care (including vision and dental care), affordable and stable housing, well-resourced public schools, and family assets that allow for long-term financial planning, including plans for college. Referring to the Coleman Report, which was written in response to the Civil Rights Act in 1964, Rossides writes, "while under-funded schools would benefit from more money, they are not likely to close the gap much between themselves and schools in affluent districts unless families in lower classes are also 'better funded.'"
7. See http://www.usc.edu/dept/education/CUE/documents/urbaned.pdf for more information on the Diversity Scorecard project.
8. For more information about the origins of the Framework for Diversity Assessment and Planning and its implementation on several campuses, see the Washington Center Fall 2004 newsletter at http://www.evergreen.edu/washcenter/newsletters.htm.
9. Number based on a review of the Department of Education database of funded Title V programs for 2002.
10. Social identities are constructed in terms of dominant and disenfranchised, and individuals usually embody a mixture of social identities. For instance, a white middle-class lesbian in the United States experiences the privileges of

being white, and the lack of privilege of being gay and female. Social identity development theory is an adaptation of black identity development theory and white identity development theory (Adams, Bell, and Griffin 1997).

11. The limits of the "just an American" view becomes evident when considering the following fact: Barack Obama is the *only* African American senator currently serving, and only the *third* in our country since Reconstruction. Merit alone, absent confounding factors of race and class, wouldn't predict that pattern of underrepresentation. In fact, Obama identifies himself as an African who is an American.

12. An assignment borrowed from Marie Ponsot and Rosemary Deen (1982), *Beat Not the Poor Desk: Writing: What to Teach, How to Teach It, and Why*.

13. Paul Kivel's, *Uprooting Racism* (2002), and Allen Johnson's, *Privilege, Power and Difference* (2001), provide additional accessible discussions of systems of privilege and power based on social identities including race, gender, and class.

14. Source: http://www.diversityweb.org/Digest/W97/currrec.html.

15. Several web sites provide useful material on curriculum transformation efforts, including Diversity Web (www.diversityweb.org), the Multicultural Pavilion (www.edchange.org/multicultural), the University of Michigan's Center for Research on Learning and Teaching (www.crlt.umich.edu/multiteaching), and the Teaching Effectiveness Program site at the University of Oregon (http://tep.uoregon.edu/resources/diversity). Marjorie Kitano (1997) has developed a useful framework outlining four dimensions of curriculum transformation, including content, instructional strategies, assessment, and classroom dynamics.

16. For program description, see http://academic.evergreen.edu/curricular/palod.

17. Source: *New York Times*, May 18, 1980.

References

Adams, M., L. A. Bell, and P. Griffin. 1997. *Teaching for Diversity and Social Justice: A Sourcebook*. New York: Routledge.

American Political Science Association, Task Force on Inequality and American Democracy. 2004. "American Democracy in an Age of Rising Inequality." Washington, D.C.

Banks, J. A. 2002. "Teaching for Diversity and Unity in a Democratic Multicultural Society." In *Education for Democracy: Contexts, Curricula, Assessments*, Vol. 2, edited by W. Parker. Greenwich, CN: Information Age Publishing.

Bartholomae, D. 1988. "Inventing the University." In *Perspectives on Literacy,* edited by E. R. Kintgen, B. M. Kroll, and M. Rose. Carbondale, IL: Southern Illinois University Press.

Beckham, E. 2004. "Diversity: An Educational Imperative." In *Engaging the Whole of Service-Learning, Diversity, and Learning Communities*, edited by Galura, J. A., P. A. Pasque, D. Schoem, and J. Howard. Ann Arbor, MI: The OCSL Press at University of Michigan; Edward Ginsberg Center for Community Service and Learning.

Bensimon, E. M. 2004. "The Diversity Scorecard: A Learning Approach to Institutional Change." *Change* 36(1), January/February: 45–52.

———, ed. 1994. *Multicultural Teaching and Learning: Strategies for Change in Higher Education*. Pennsylvania State University: National Center on Postsecondary Teaching, Learning, and Assessment.

Bok, Derek. 2003. "Closing the Nagging Gap in Minority Achievement." *Chronicle of Higher Education* October 24: B20.

Cajete, G. 1994. *Look to the Mountain: An Ecology of Indigenous Education*. Skyland, NC: Kivaki Press.

Cornwell, G., and E. W. Stoddard. 1999. *Globalizing Knowledge: Connecting International & Intercultural Studies*. The Academy in Transition Series. Washington, D.C.: Association of American Colleges and Universities.

Dewey, J. 1916. *Democracy and Education*. New York: Free Press.

———. 1927. *The Public and Its Problems*. Denver: Alan Swallow.

———. 1931. "American Education Past and Future." In *John Dewey: The Later Works, 1925–1953 Volume 6: 1931–1932*, edited by J. A. Boydston. Carbondale, IL: Southern Illinois University Press.

———. Address delivered at the twenty-third Annual Conference of the National Association for the Advancement of Colored People, Washington D.C., May 19, 1932.

Du Bois, W. E. B. 1903. *The Souls of Black Folk*. Chicago: A. C. McClurg & Co.

Eaton, M., J. MacGregor, and D. Schoem. 2003. "The Educational Promise of Service-Learning Communities." In *Integrating Learning Communities with Service-Learning*, edited by J. MacGregor. National Learning Communities Project Monograph Series. Olympia, WA: The Evergreen State College, Washington Center for Improving the Quality of Undergraduate Education, in cooperation with the American Association for Higher Education.

Evelyn, J. 2003. "The 'Silent Killer' of Minority Enrollments." *The Chronicle of Higher Education* 49 (41).

Fischel, A., and L. Nelson. 2002. "Local Knowledge in the Age of Globalization." *Washington Center News*, Fall: 31–34.

Freire, P. 1998. *Pedagogy of Freedom: Ethics, Democracy, and Civic Courage*. Lanham, MD: Rowman & Littlefield Publishers, Inc.

García Márquez, G. "The Solitude of Latin America." Nobel Lecture, December 8, 1982.

Gonzalez, J. 2000. *Harvest of Empire: A History of Latinos in America*. New York: Penguin Books.

Graff, G. 1992. *Beyond Culture Wars: How Teaching the Conflicts Can Revitalize American Education*. New York: W. W. Norton & Company.

Harding, S. 1991. *Whose Science? Whose Knowledge? Thinking from Women's Lives*. Ithaca, NY: Cornell University Press.

Hill, P. n.d. "Community, Power and Diversity: Reflections and Caveats on Learning Communities." Unpublished manuscript.

Howell, A., and F. Tuitt. 2003. *Race and Higher Education: Rethinking Pedagogy in Diverse College Classrooms*. Cambridge, MA: Harvard Graduate School of Education.

Hurtado, S. 1996. "How Diversity Affects Teaching and Learning: Climate of Inclusion Has a Positive Effect on Learning Outcomes." *The Educational Record*, 77(4), Fall: 27–29.

Hurtado, S., J. Milem, A. Clayton-Pedersen, and W. Allen. 1999. *Enacting Diverse Learning Environments: Improving the Climate for Racial/Ethnic Diversity in Higher Education*. ASHE-ERIC Higher Education Report 26(8). Washington D.C.: The George Washington University, Graduate School of Education and Human Development.

Ibarra, R. A. 2001. *Beyond Affirmative Action: Reframing the Context of Higher Education*. Madison, WI: University of Wisconsin Press.

Kazis, R., J. Vargas, and N. Hoffman, eds. 2004. *Double the Numbers: Increasing Postsecondary Credentials for Underrepresented Youth*. Cambridge, MA: Harvard Education Press.

Kitano, M. K. 1997. "A Rationale and Framework for Course Change." In *Multicultural Course Transformation in Higher Education*, edited by A. I. Morey and M. K. Kitano. Needham Heights, MA: Allyn and Bacon.

Lamkin, M. D. 2004. "More Money is Not Enough: Philanthropy Can Play a Unique Role in Providing Greater Access and Affordability in Higher Education." *Notebook*, Winter: 2.

Lardner, E. 2004. "Approaching Diversity Through Learning Communities." In *Sustaining and Improving Learning Communities* by J. Levine Laufgraben, N. Shapiro, and Associates. San Francisco: Jossey-Bass.

Levine Laufgraben, J., N. Shapiro, and Associates. 2004. *Sustaining and Improving Learning Communities*. San Francisco: Jossey-Bass.

Loo, C. M., and G. Rolison. 1986. "Alienation of Ethnic Minority Students at a Predominately White University." *Journal of Higher Education* 57: 58–77.

Malnarich, G. 2005. "Learning Communities and Curricular Reform: 'Academic Apprenticeships' for Developmental Students." In *Responding to the Challenges of Developmental Education*, edited by C. A. Kozeracki. New Directions for Community Colleges, Spring, No. 129. San Francisco: Jossey-Bass.

Malnarich, G., with others. 2003. *The Pedagogy of Possibilities: Developmental Education, College-Level Studies, and Learning Communities*. National Learning Communities Project Monograph Series. Olympia, WA: The Evergreen State College, Washington Center for Improving the Quality of Undergraduate Education, in cooperation with the American Association of Community Colleges.

Malnarich, G., and E. Lardner. 2003. "Designing Integrated Learning for Students: A Heuristic for Teaching, Assessment, and Curriculum Design." *Washington Center Occasional Paper*, Winter No. 1. Olympia, WA: The Washington Center for Improving the Quality of Undergraduate Education.

McIntosh, P. 1988. "White Privilege and Male Privilege: A Personal Account of Coming to See Correspondences Through Work in Women's Studies." Working Paper No.189. Wellesley, MA: Wellesley College, Center for Research on Women.

Moses, R., and C. E. Cobb, Jr. 2001. *Radical Equations: Civil Rights from Mississippi to the Algebra Project*. Boston, MA: Beacon Press.

Nieto, S. 1999. *The Light in Their Eyes: Creating Multicultural Learning Communities*. New York: Teachers College Press.

Nossoff, J., and D. Young. 2004. "Multiple Models of Learning Community Seminars at a Research University." In *Integrating the First-Year Experience: The Role of First-Year Seminars in Learning Communities*, edited by J. Henscheid. Columbia, SC: University of South Carolina, National Resource Center for The First-Year Experience and Students in Transition.

Nussbaum, M. 2003. "Compassion & Terror." *Daedalus*, Winter 132(1): 10–26.

———. 1997. *Cultivating Humanity: A Classical Defense of Reform in Liberal Education*. Cambridge, MA: Harvard University Press.

O'Brien, E. M., and C. Zudak. 1998. "Minority Serving Institutions: An Overview." In *Minority-Serving Institutions: Distinct Purposes, Common Goals*, edited by J. P. Merisotis and C. T. O'Brien. New Directions for Higher Education, no. 102. San Francisco: Jossey-Bass.

Parson, W. L. 2002. "In Retrospect: 1996–2001 Excerpt From a Faculty Five Year Self-Evaluation." *Washington Center News*, Fall: 8–10.

Pascarella, E. T., and P. T. Terenzini. 1991. *How College Affects Students*. San Francisco: Jossey-Bass.

Ponsot, M., and R. Deen. 1982. *Beat Not the Poor Desk: Writing: What to Teach, How to Teach It, and Why*. Montclair, NJ: Boynton/Cook Publishers, Inc.

Rendón, L. 2004. "Transforming the First-Year Experience for Students of Color: Where Do We Begin?" In *Transforming the First-Year Experience for Students of Color*, Monograph No. 38, edited by L. I. Rendón, M. García, and D. Person. Columbia, SC: University of South Carolina, National Resource Center for The First-Year Experience and Students in Transition.

Rendón, L. I., M. García, and D. Person, eds. 2004. *Transforming the First-Year Experience for Students of Color*, Monograph No. 38. Columbia, SC: University of South Carolina, National Resource Center for The First-Year Experience and Students in Transition.

Rossides, D. W. 2004. "Knee-Jerk Formalism: Reforming American Education." *The Journal of Higher Education* 75(6).

Rothstein, R. 2004. "The Achievement Gap: A Broader Picture." *Education Leadership* 62(3): 40–43.

Shaunghnessy, M. P. 1977. *Errors & Expectations: A Guide for the Teacher of Basic Writing*. New York: Oxford University Press.

Shulman, L. S. 2004. *Teaching as Community Property: Essays on Higher Education*. San Francisco: Jossey-Bass.

———. 2001. "The Challenge of Learning Communities as a Growing National Movement." *Peer Review*, Summer/Fall: 4-8.

Smith, B. L., J. MacGregor, R. S. Matthews, and F. Gabelnick. 2004. *Learning Communities: Reforming Undergraduate Education*. San Francisco: Jossey-Bass.

Smith, M., D. Ward, C. Willermet, and D. Guerrero. 2004. "Building Integrated Learning Experiences at a Bi-National, Commuter Institution." In *Integrating the First-Year Experience: The Role of Seminars in Learning Communities*, Monograph 39, edited J. Henscheid. Columbia, SC: University of South Carolina, National Resource Center for the First-Year Experience and Students in Transition.

Smitherman, G., and V. Villanueva, eds. 2003. *Language Diversity in the Classroom: From Intention to Practice*. Carbondale: Southern Illinois University Press.

Steele, C. M. 1992. "Race and the Schooling of Black Americans." *The Atlantic Monthly*, April: 68–78.

Taylor, K., et al. 2003. *Learning Community Research and Assessment: What We Know Now*. National Learning Communities Project Monograph Series. Olympia, WA: The Evergreen State College, Washington Center for Improving the Quality of Undergraduate Education, in cooperation with the American Association for Higher Education.

Tierney, W. G. 1992. "An Anthropological Analysis of Student Participation in College." *Journal of Higher Education*, November/December, 63(6).

Tinto, V., A. Goodsell-Love, and P. Russo. 1993. "Building Community." *Journal of Liberal Education*, Fall:16-21.

Vasques-Scalera, C. 2002. "The Diversity Framework Informing This Volume." In *Included in Communication: Learning Climates That Cultivate Racial and Ethnic Diversity*, edited by J. Trent. Washington D.C.: American Association for Higher Education in cooperation with the National Communication Association.

Vorrath, H. H., and L. K. Brendtro. 1985. *Positive Peer Culture*. New York: Aldine Publishing Company.

Washington, J. M, ed. 1986. *A Testament of Hope: The Essential Writings and Speeches of Martin Luther King Jr*. New York: HarperCollins.

Zull, J. E. 2002. *The Art of Changing the Brain: Enriching the Practice of Teaching by Exploring the Biology of Learning*. Sterling, VA: Stylus Publishing.

Emily Lardner co-directs the Washington Center for Improving the Quality of Undergraduate Education at The Evergreen State College and teaches academic writing in the Evening/Weekend Studies program.

(In)Visibility: Teaching Diversity on an "Homogeneous" Campus

Heather Keast and Barbara Williamson

Living and teaching at a predominantly white college with a predominantly white faculty in a predominantly white city, the task of teaching about diversity begins with a question of "why": why is diversity important? Staring back at us on the first day of our classes are groups of people who generally look homogeneous; students looking around our classrooms see others, including their teachers, who look "just like" them. Although as instructors we are aware that diversity is present, because students often conflate diversity with race, and see the faces that surround them mirror their own, many students find no need to talk about diversity because it appears to be absent. In this situation, when we teachers invoke "diversity," students react as if we somehow are *creating* a problem. Diversity as a concept has become oversimplified and strictly "academic." Consequently, we turn to the underlying problem: students' complacency in the face of the diversity that is present, albeit invisible and often marginalized, that is, sexual orientation.

To further complicate matters, students' early anti-racist education has programmed them with a mantra that, because we are all human, if difference does exist, it doesn't matter. As a result, we often hear "I don't see color" or "Women can do anything men can do." Many elements of identity are erased by this assimilative tactic—gender, sexual orientation, age, class, experience, even ultimately race itself. What diversity there is in the classroom is collapsed under the pressure of the dominant culture belief that one must ignore difference in order to combat racism. In addition, students whose diversity is more marginalized remain hidden due to perceived, and too often real, intolerance toward that "type" of diversity. This intolerance, based on the deepest held religious and cultural beliefs and perpetuated in traditional family and educational structures, can be the most subtle threat to achieving educational equity. For example, dominant culture, heterosexual students feel free to release their most homophobic thoughts because they are in a classroom of like-looking (and therefore like-minded) individuals; they might even be proud of their heterosexism, wielding it as a badge of honor that marks them as morally superior. Although most students of color on our campus are relatively assured that they won't be blatantly attacked in our classrooms, such assurance is not available to students whose diversity is more invisible. As Hoffman, Bakken, and Stone contend, "due to homophobia, students who are struggling with their sexual orientation may not be able to learn while they are attending class; rather, these students must learn how to survive" (2001, 76).

Furthermore, lesbian and gay students often have internalized cultural homophobia, turning their own diversity into a source of pain and contributing to their need to cloak their identities. The more adept these students are at manipulating what W. E. B. Du Bois (1903) calls "double-consciousness," the more adept they are at blending in and playing the dominant culture game, the more culturally invisible they become. The more invisible they become, the more difficult is our task of disrupting simplistic notions of diversity. As these problems compound, the task of teaching students about the diversity that surrounds us becomes even more difficult. Although for this examination we've narrowed our focus to addressing sexual orientation, this aspect of diversity is merely one face of the larger issue of oppression in our world. While the multi-layered, complex nature of oppression makes it "virtually impossible to view one oppression . . . in isolation because they are all connected: sexism, racism, homophobia, classism, ableism, anti-Semitism, ageism" (Pharr 1988, 53), attempting a more limited scope does allow for an easier entrance into the murky issues surrounding the teaching of diversity. Learning communities, because of their unique structure, offer an ideal environment for deconstructing narrower notions of diversity and creating a more inclusive definition, one that accounts for the complexity of diversity present even in an all-white classroom.

Because so much of the learning that takes place in a learning community is dependent on community, instructors and students must take time to establish and nurture it. This emphasis eventually translates into a classroom where students and teachers are secure enough to confront hard issues. Like bell hooks (1994), we believe that teaching requires a "transformative space" that often is not safe, but we must begin by establishing a level of comfort from which students may venture. Whereas in a stand-alone class we might spend an hour or two throughout the quarter fostering relationships, in a learning community this fostering becomes a focus. In the first week of our learning community pairing American literature with three levels of composition, we begin like many instructors with an opening day icebreaker in which each student must learn surprising facts about his or her peers that separate each student from the others in the class. An example we will always remember is our student of several years ago, Steve, who was run over by a golf cart. Although most of the facts reported are silly and humorous, what does emerge is a sense that despite our homogeneous appearance, the forty-seven people in the class are unique. The fact may seem obvious but, when highlighted, it begins to quietly disrupt "sameness," the notion that sustains an invisibility ultimately dangerous to lesbian and gay students. As Connie Chan points out, "The greatest obstacle to combating heterosexism is the invisibility of lesbian, gay, and bisexual issues [and] individuals . . . on campuses" (1996, 27). While such an exercise in establishing difference does little to bring gay issues to the forefront specifically, it does allow difference to take center stage in the classroom.

Lest these differences, small though they may be, drive a budding community into individual isolation, after finding out several unique facts about each student, we ask students to get together in groups of four or five people whom they did not know before the class began, and discover a quality or characteristic that binds the members of this small group together yet distinguishes the group from the rest of the class. Having accomplished this, they name their group "We Who ____," filling in the blank with their group's identity. For instance, one group chose the name "We Who Eat Pizza with Forks," while another chose the name "We Who Have Never Been to the Ocean." Once their group identity is established, each group and its members are introduced to the class, explaining the significance of its name and how they came to find it. This juxtaposition of finding difference and similarity within our own learning community serves as a microcosm of the diversity work we will continue throughout the quarter. The next day, we establish two other types of quarterlong groups: seminar and book club. From their first meetings with each group, students must work together to accomplish a given task, be it brainstorming discussion expectations in seminar or planning a reading schedule in book club, thus establishing the foundation for communal learning intrinsic to the course.

Each type of group—named, seminar, and book—is made up of different students. Each student belongs to three distinct groups with three different sets of students, and each group has ongoing opportunities to bond over the course of the quarter. Beyond the many learning opportunities such bonds create, the simple opportunity to develop sustained relationships with many people throughout the quarter promotes "the identification of similarities in values and beliefs [and] also enhances mutual understanding and liking. Since these factors are not compatible with hostility, their presence produces a decrease in prejudice" (Lance 2002, 414), a valuable goal in itself. In our paired class, then, in the first week alone, we spend six to eight hours establishing community, in contrast to two hours over the course of the entire quarter in our stand-alone classes. Additionally, students feel a part of several micro-communities, each of which is designed to both challenge and support them. Most important, from the first day of class, students are forced to confront their assumptions that a safe space is based on sameness, and that if someone looks like them, they must believe like them. From the first day of class, establishing community becomes about confronting the assumptions upon which the equation of safety to sameness is based. Because of the varying characteristics of their groups and the unique make-up of each, each space can be "safe" in different ways.

Once we have begun to establish a community that disrupts the simplistic thinking that visual homogeneity equals hegemony, the next hurdle comes with a tendency to "tokenize" the diversity that is now becoming apparent. Again, learning communities provide the perfect forum for combating this tendency. In an ideal learning community, each student becomes irreplaceable, an integral part of the learning process. To borrow Jim Harnish's instructions to his seminar students, the learning community "should be a better place because you were there." The value placed on the individual student has two effects. In the first, each student, and whatever diversity he or she brings to the table, feels a valuable part of the community. In the second, each individual is individual*ized*, so that his or her knowledge is not artificially forced to represent the attitudes of entire groups of people. Because students spend so much time getting to know each other, each student becomes more fully human and less a compendium of characteristics, which mitigates the tendency to require a particular student to speak for an entire group.

An examination of a seminar discussion demonstrates this "anti-tokenizing" force of community. Early in the quarter, during a seminar in which Adrienne Rich's poetry was being examined, students were intrigued by the relationship between Rich's biography and her writing. In fact, her lesbianism became the overriding issue in seminar, subsuming not only her writing but all other aspects of her identity as well, perhaps due to the students' lack of exposure to issues of sexual diversity. Although some students tried to steer the conversation back to Rich's poetry, the seminar kept circling back to Rich's sexual orientation. Throughout the seminar, several students turned and addressed Katy, an out lesbian, specifically, asking, "Why would lesbians get married in the first place?" and "Why do lesbians hate men?" Understandably frustrated, Katy snapped back, "Lesbians don't hate men." Her seminar mate then replied, "You don't have to be so sensitive." Even though the experience was uncomfortable for Katy (and others as well), during seminar debriefing the next day, Katy volunteered what it felt like when she was asked to speak for all lesbians. She recognized that no malice was intended on the part of her seminar companions; they simply had not thought about what it was they were doing.

Katy's ability to speak about being forced into the role of "the token lesbian" allowed others in our class to see how being placed in such a position unfairly truncated Katy's own voice and inappropriately forced her to counter the negative stereotypes aired. Through discussion, students came to see Katy's double-bind: if she spoke up, she tokenized herself by speaking on behalf of "her people"; if she didn't speak, she allowed the perpetuation of negative stereotypes. Because she functions on the margins of dominance, Katy was well aware of the political ramifications of voice whereas the dominant culture students in the class, having the luxury of a perceived hegemony, had never *needed* to be aware of the politics of discourse. As David Wallace reminds us:

> [T]he problem for many people who have no experience in speaking/reading/acting as 'others' is that the performative nature of discourse is not readily visible. Because their experiences with discourse have not consistently placed them in positions in which they need to speak back to cultural values that define them in problematic ways, they have difficulty understanding why others must do so. Thus, for many people, the ideologies of culture and discourse appear neutral and their sense of agency as relatively unencumbered. (2002, 53)

In a learning community, then, through individualized contact, students begin to recognize the "ideologies of culture" and deconstruct their neutrality; they begin to see why others must speak for themselves but not for entire classes of people. Through building community, students begin to break down the tendency toward false representation and see each other as complex individuals, characterized by difference but not limited to it. Students become better equipped to deconstruct preconceptions and reconstruct more complex ideas, both with their peers and on their own, regarding a multitude of topics, diversity being just one of them.

This safe space forms a foundation to both learning communities and to the teaching of diversity—particularly when addressing homophobia and heterosexism—that enables students to generate knowledge both communally and individually. Because learning communities deliberately move the teachers from the center of the classroom, knowledge becomes more of a shared phenomenon, as all participants become more aware of the social process of knowledge creation. Learning community students must become more participatory. They must construct and deconstruct knowledge in an authentically recursive process. Rather than *delivered* as in a traditional classroom, knowledge is *arrived at.* So, to return to the example of Katy, students weren't handed a definition of tokenization from on high and told it was "bad"; rather, as a class they experienced the phenomenon and learned in a more authentic (and risky) manner. Rather than listening to a teacher talk about tokenization and then preparing to regurgitate that information for a test, knowledge tied to actual experience transformed them (Kitano 1997). Additionally, because that knowledge is self- and peer-generated, it reduces the threat factor that occurs when fundamental belief structures are challenged. Students don't have to retreat because they aren't being attacked from the outside. Finally, because students share in the generation of new knowledge, they share more responsibility for its development and internalization. As such, it carries more weight. It is more authentic, more applicable to their own lives, more real to them.

The function of this self-generated knowledge emerges as well through an examination of student book clubs, a "faculty-free" space designed to allow students to take responsibility for their own learning and the learning of their peers, thus empowering students to find their own voices. In our American literature paired with composition class, for instance, students selected novels to be read in small groups from a list that included books by an Indian American woman, an African American lesbian, a Native American woman, a working class European American man, as well as a middle-class European American male academic. Our goal was to introduce students to voices reflecting a range of social identities and to their own voices as writers, to explore what it means to be an American.

Despite these opportunities for students to select from a range of writers, and despite our prompting that they choose something not in their "comfort zone," the two reading groups focusing on books by white males filled first; the books expressing diversity in its traditional form, race, filling next; and the book dealing with the diversity that might actually *be* in their classroom—sexual orientation—filling last. The students who were ultimately placed in the group reading *Zami: A New Spelling of My Name* by Audre Lorde, were a mixed bag: a European-American 16-year-old heterosexual male; a European American 18-year-old heterosexual female; a 35-year-old Hispanic closeted lesbian; and a 22-year-old European American bisexual woman. Only the 35-year-old had chosen the book as her first choice, and because we were reluctant to push people into such a potentially polarizing situation, we did not "fill out" the club with students who selected *Zami* lower than second on their list of choices.

When the quarter began, as is typical with beginning students, the student-written discussion questions (required before each week's meeting) were very superficial and tenuous, skating as far as possible from the heart of the book. For instance, "Do you like the book so far?" was a typical question. As the quarter progressed and the students in the club were forced to grapple on their own with the multiple oppressions expressed in the book as Lorde flips focus from lesbians to black Americans to women without allowing her readers to dismiss any one social identity, the students in the club became markedly more thoughtful, asking questions like "How does the fact that she's black and a lesbian and a woman and first generation work together to create her identity?" and "What is the function of storytelling in identity creation?" As the quarter moved along and the students began to discuss how they would present the book to the class, a requirement for successful completion of their club, their discussions became richer and more complex. They wrestled with the intersection of oppression and privilege and various ways to communicate that complexity to their peers. The students in this group engaged in a process of ongoing self-generating knowledge, and ultimately, the book became a platform for the most engaging final presentation, a presentation reminiscent of Jane Elliot's "Blue Eyes, Brown Eyes" exercise.

On the day of the presentation, we were not allowed to enter the classroom as usual; instead, as folks arrived, some were randomly given ribbons to wear around their arms. They were then allowed into the classroom while those without ribbons waited without explanation outside the doors. Once we were all allowed inside, we were put into "neighborhoods," and in each neighborhood, the beribboned were accorded various subtle and blatant privileges. While the rest of the class watched what was going on, each neighborhood participated in an activity designed to highlight the inequality between sets of people. After all the activities, the book club students led a discussion about privilege and the way it functions in everyday life. Further, they asked students to reflect on how having a ribbon or not having a ribbon felt. For many beribboned students, it was the first time they had become aware of the notion of privilege in an immediate, albeit artificial, way. Many of our mostly dominant culture students had not only never experienced discrimination before but had not realized the ways they themselves had actively, if unconsciously, perpetrated discrimination. In particular, one beribboned student who had tried to refuse ice cream when others were not allowed to eat and who had been pressured not to refuse by other ribbon-wearers around her reported feeling discomfort, even disgust, at not being able to discard her privilege. Other ribbon-wearers reported feeling protective of their status, as when one wanted to make sure that all non-wearers had a clean-up job to do before "volunteering" to help clean up as well. Non-wearers reported feelings of anger at the ribbon-wearers, while still others wanted to know how they could earn a ribbon.

The book club students then led a discussion that allowed us to see that the issuing of ribbons had been an arbitrary process; those with them had done nothing to earn them while those without had merely happened into that situation, much like sexual orientation or race or gender, which is not chosen but simply randomly "assigned." Additionally, while we could discard our ribbons—and the benefits and drawbacks of them—as we walked out the door, other privileges, like heterosexual privilege, stay with the bearers and cannot be discarded. The book club students acknowledged the artificiality of the situation but asked us to extrapolate the situation to real, lifelong, inescapable conditions. During the course of the presentation, all students were engaged in the process of generating knowledge; everyone in the classroom learned to reflect on these important issues. In fact, the students voted this presentation "most thought-provoking." Students walked away from this presentation, and several others that week, with a much deeper sense of the pressures of marginalization. While book clubs are a practice that can be integrated into stand-alone classes, the possibilities for self- and communally-generated knowledge building on each other are greater in a learning community than in a stand-alone course.

Learning to generate knowledge is clearly a valuable experience in itself; however, the distinct type of knowledge generated by a learning community classroom allows students to more fully deconstruct homophobia and heterosexism. Because dominant culture perpetuates its power by maintaining a focus on individual discrimination, beginning college students often feel challenged in understanding the multifaceted nature of systemic oppression, having only thought about oppression—if they thought of it at all—in terms of individualized discrimination. Also, recognizing oppression as systemic is viewed as almost antithetical to an "American" sensibility given the cultural emphasis on the individual as the locus of control. By nature of the interconnections of their disciplines, learning communities model the types of complex thinking necessary to conceptualize and engage with notions of systemic oppression. In order to make connections between disparate disciplines, students in learning communities must develop higher-level thinking skills that help them to see the intersection of the disciplines in question. Instructors can then utilize these skills to complicate students' thinking about diversity as well.

For example, in a learning community combining sociology, literature, and composition, we regularly asked students to apply the sociological paradigms they were learning to the literature they were reading. To better understand how gender is socialized, for instance, we asked them to investigate the strategies used to succumb to, reascribe, pass on, or resist gender roles in the poetry we had read. In our class combining global social problems, ecology, and composition, students drew a sociological issue from a hat, chose an environmental problem they were interested in, and used the country they had focused on in a previous paper to make a connection between a global sociological issue and an environmental problem. Both assignments asked students to make connections between disciplines. In the first example, falling toward the beginning of the quarter, students had to develop a connection we named for them whereas in the second example, which came near the end of the quarter, we asked students to make connections for themselves. What these assignments have in common is the deliberate bringing together of ideas across disciplines to investigate questions and issues in the world. Although these assignments don't target an examination of oppression specifically, as students gain facility in this type of meaning-making, they become better able to recognize and deconstruct the connections that bind oppressions together as well.

Once students have become more adept at navigating the critical pathways needed to conceptualize a complicated view of diversity, learning communities can be designed in ways that invite students to notice entrenched patterns of "centrisms." Learning to build connections between voices and ideas is a first step in breaking down the isolationist "us" and "them" thinking that perpetuates oppression. Again, because of the unique nature of a cross-disciplinary learning community, those alternate patterns of thinking are embedded in the curriculum, waiting to be activated. In our learning community pairing American literature and composition, for instance, we structured the class around an examination of the multiplicity of "American" as a concept, consciously including voices of diverse genders, sexual orientations, immigrant statuses, economic statuses, and ages as well as races, thus making it virtually impossible *not* to confront diversity on multiple levels. Set up as a series of dialogues, our texts deliberately spoke to notions of "American" from several perspectives. Our core texts, those we read as an entire class, were fairly canonical, several written by white, heterosexual male authors; our book club choices, as well as other core texts, introduced alternative voices into the dialogue. Having read Chopin's version of the cult of domesticity and Rich's reaction to the 1950s version of that cult, for instance, students in seminar deepened their understanding of the place of women in literary history by contrasting these two visions, by looking at how "woman" fits into "American." Additionally, because our women writers were so different from one another, several students began to examine the validity of "woman" as a category in itself, arguing that due to the diversity in female voices, "woman" as a category had little meaning.

In another dialogue, we book-ended our course with two contrasting visions of the ramifications of American slavery, a white male perspective in *The Adventures of Huckleberry Finn* and an African American female perspective in *Beloved.* By placing these texts in dialogue, discussing and writing about them in community with one another, we came to see a wider, more complex vision of "American" than we would have had reading canonical texts in a stand-alone class. Furthermore, the luxury of time afforded by linking classes allowed students in a book club to discover other connections; for instance, a contrast between the way Bharati Mukherjee conceptualizes "American," and Hemingway's conception of "American."

Because students had to share their newfound knowledge in community with others through writing and discussing, allowing others' insights to deepen and solidify their own, they learned to think complexly. Again and again students told us that, having believed they had thoroughly prepared for seminar, having read the texts and written the required seminar paper, they would return home after seminar to rewrite the entire paper because they now understood so much more deeply than before. One student told us that it was as if seminar were a mirror he stepped through to enter an entirely new world of knowledge, and that world required a more complex set of eyes. This multiplicity of perspectives, highlighting the dynamic and fluid nature of knowledge, emerges in a learning community through shared discourse. The skills students use to create this knowledge belong to the same set of skills that are necessary to begin to understand the complexity inherent in notions of systemic oppression of all types. In fact, when students engage on this level, when they learn to think critically about the world around them, they turn to examinations of diversity almost organically as they attempt to sort out a world made richer by the differences surrounding them.

When diversity is more complicated than "race," other dimensions of diversity become visible. Because a learning community is a politicized space, its very structure deconstructs neutrality, allowing students to see that, as Mary Elliot points out, ". . . the classroom is never a 'neutral' space. Neutrality . . . is a universal cultural default setting which is almost always presumed to be heterosexual and white; it is not available to those who cannot 'pass' as either or both" (1996, 698). In attenuating students to this "cultural default setting," learning communities move students beyond their own comfort zones into what Emily Lardner calls epistemological humility, a growing recognition of the partiality of any one perspective on the world that enables them to grapple more effectively with diversity issues. Learning communities can be intentionally designed to help break open even a relatively monochromatic campus to reveal a much more "colorful" picture, one that moves beyond skin color to better reflect the realities of the richly textured communities in which we live. As the pluralism inherent in the larger community becomes visible within the safety of the learning community classroom, the ways in which learners exercise their white (and dominant culture) privileges are mitigated. The exposure of pluralism where none appears visible answers the "why" question: diversity education is important because people who look like you are not always like you. When pluralism is exposed within a learning community, students have a safe space inside which they may grapple with difficult issues, a space where diversity can be recognized and engaged—no longer ignored and certainly not simply tolerated.

References

Chan, C. 1996. "Combating Heterosexism in Educational Institutions: Structural Changes and Strategies." In E. D. Rothblum & L. A. Bord, eds., *Preventing Heterosexism and Homophobia*: 20–35. Thousand Oaks, CA: Sage.

Du Bois, W. E. B. 1903. *The Souls of Black Folk*. Chicago: A. C. McClurg, & Co.

Elliot, M. 1996. "Coming Out in the Classroom: A Return to the Hard Place." *College English*, 58: 693–708.

Hoffman, A., L. Bakken, and B. Stone. 2001. "Are Educational and Life Experiences Related to Homophobia?" *Educational Research Quarterly*, 24(4): 67–82.

hooks, bell. 1994. *Teaching to Transgress: Education as the Practice of Freedom*. New York: Routledge.

Kitano, M. K. 1997. "What a Course Will Look Like After Multicultural Change." In *Multicultural Course Transformation in Higher Education: A Broader Truth*, edited by A. I. Morey and M. K. Kitano. Boston, MA: Allyn and Bacon.

Lance, L. M. 2002. "Heterosexism and Homophobia Among College Students." *College Student Journal*, 36, 411–19.

Lardner, E., and others. 2005. *Diversity, Educational Equity, and Learning Communities*. Learning Communities & Educational Reform, Summer. Olympia, WA: The Evergreen State College, Washington Center for Improving the Quality of Undergraduate Education.

Pharr, S. 1988. *Homophobia: A Weapon of Sexism*. Little Rock, AR: Chardon.

Wallace, D. 2002. "Out in the Academy: Heterosexism, Invisibility, and Double Consciousness." *College English,* 65: 53–66.

Heather Keast and Barbara Williamson are English instructors at Spokane Falls Community College. Williamson also coordinates the learning community program.

Nurturing the "Whole Person": The Learning Community Experience as a Safe Space

Carol Hamilton and Jane Lister Reis

It is fall quarter 2003 and forty-one students[1] have signed up for an evening coordinated studies course at North Seattle Community College. The first night of any coordinated studies course is typically the same—students sitting quietly at their desks waiting patiently to be told what is expected of them. There is little personal interaction, no small talk. The room is quiet; the students are separated and subdued. It is something that we, as the instructors, hope will change as a result of their participation in this learning community.

This change—from passive, separated learners to engaged, even excited, learners—is something we believe will happen organically *if* we can provide the right balance of academic rigor and relational community-building ingredients. The purpose of this article is to share three practices that we have learned to incorporate into our learning community if we want to foster this kind of holistic or "whole person" learning experience for students and ourselves.

Beginnings has been offered at NSCC, both a day and evening section, as part of the fall integrated studies course offerings for the last several years, and was specifically designed to offer support for new and returning students to the community college experience. This year's course theme is *Beginnings: Finding Our Voice, Communicating with Each Other through Stories* and it is being taught by a full-time English faculty member and a part-time Communications faculty member. This coordinated studies course combines composition, multicultural literature, intercultural communication, and a survey of basic communication competency (interpersonal, small group communication, and oral presentation) for a total of twelve credit hours.

The course's learning goals are directly linked to the college's student learning outcomes. The course's uniqueness, however, is shaped by both instructors' shared personal belief and historical faith in the "transformative" learning experience where the development of an intellectually *and* emotionally safe community is as important as academic rigor. We have found that when we are able to create this delicate mix of openness to new ideas and high academic standards with opportunities for honesty, personal voice, and reflection, the learning experience provides all participants, students and teachers, with surprising moments of wisdom and learning. It is as if this mixture creates an academic womb that nourishes and fosters growth for all.

As educators, our belief and trust in the creation of safe learning spaces has been influenced by the women's movement, in particular by the academic research and writings of Carol Gilligan and Mary Field Belenky, who have written about the development of women's voices and the creation of "public homeplaces," and also from our own extensive involvement in reflective practices and women's circles. Our understanding of a safe space very much mirrors Mary Field Belenky, Lynne Bond, and Jacqueline Weinstock's definition of a "public homeplace":

> Public homeplaces are places where people support each other's development and where everyone is expected to participate in developing the homeplace. Using the homeplace as a model, the members go on working to make the whole society more inclusive, nurturing, and responsive to the developmental needs of all people—but most especially to those who have been excluded and silenced. (1999, 13)

As we began to plan our course to support our theme of story, voice, and identity, we intentionally designed an eclectic blend of assignments for the students to interact with: regular reading and writing about the texts that were discussed in weekly seminars and writing workshops; practicing a variety of multicultural, small group, and interpersonal communication exercises; listening to different guest speakers; watching an assortment of videos; participating in a group research project and giving an oral presentation; and finally, submitting a final individual portfolio coupled with a self-evaluation. This last assignment gave students an opportunity to reflect on their experience in the course, on the knowledge they developed, and the skills they improved in the areas of writing, reading, group work, research, and communication (interpersonal, multicultural, and public presentation).

The texts we chose were critical to the course. Because we believed it was important to provide a cultural framework that would support a rich discussion on the process of learning about our own identities, and provide a way to share our own stories, we chose: *Privilege, Power, and Difference,* a theoretical text on white privilege by Allan Johnson (a white, heterosexual male); *Where the Body Meets Memory: An Odyssey of Race, Sexuality, and Identity,* a cultural identity memoir written by David Mura (a Japanese American male); and three cultural novels—*Dreaming in Cuban* by Christina Garcia (a Cuban American female), *Love Medicine by* Louise Erdrich (a Native American female), and *Mama Day* by Gloria Naylor (an African American female).

Practicing Honesty

Our first step towards intentionally creating an inclusive and safe learning community was honesty. We began with the hypothesis that we don't know each other's cultures and stories, and asked why. We started with white privilege and racism. By the end of the first week of class, we had watched the highly intense video "The Color of Fear" (the first of the two videos by filmmaker Lee Mun Wah, a nationally known diversity consultant and "community" therapist), discussed Peggy McIntosh's article "White Privilege: Unpacking the Invisible Knapsack," and read Allan Johnson's book on white privilege. These three choices immediately forced us as an entire class to see, discuss, and listen to the painful impact racism has on people of color and to become aware of the obliviousness many white people have about their social privilege and unconscious participation in perpetuating racism. Although many students were shocked, our decision to begin in this way put in place a pedagogical framework that would shape the rest of the quarter. By beginning with what has separated us, we hoped to build upon this honesty and define the heart of our learning community as a place where all voices and stories would be respected. Here, from their final portfolios, are what some students said about this immediate plunge into understanding privilege and difference and its impact on them as co-learners in the class:

> Learning about white privilege has been difficult, but enlightening and necessary. The first thing I noticed after reading Johnson's book was the many ways that I benefit from white privilege. For example, I started to notice that people of color get treated as if they are invisible, including by me. I was saddened and shocked by my own behavior, so I decided to make a conscious effort to change it. Instead of making judgments in my mind, I now try to recognize my thinking, and then alter it. When I am able to do this, the results are

> wonderful. I feel connected to people in a way that I never have. (White student, female)
>
> I must admit that when we first started reading the Johnson text, I was a little taken aback. The area of privilege that I most resisted was the idea that just being white allowed me a certain status and advantages that were not enjoyed by those who were not. At the time, I had very little insight into what was the motivating factor in my resistance to this idea. There were parts of my past that I had been unwilling to examine because they were too painful. As we progressed in the reading, it became clearer to me that I would need to examine my history to get to the root of my resistance. (White student, male)

Developing Personal Voice

Our second step in the development of a safe learning space was the encouragement of the development of personal voice. Our second book, David Mura's disturbingly honest portrayal, *Where Body Meets Memory,* chronicles a person of color's struggle through sexual addiction to white women as his path to discover and affirm his identity as a Japanese American male. Mura's willingness to tell his truth about personal voice, honesty, courage, and what it takes for many of us to come to terms with our cultural identity, set the bar high for us as a class. For some students, Mura gave them permission to test their voice and examine their lives in courageous ways:

> I learned a lot about my voice as a writer, because I had the freedom to express my emotions and ideas without feeling judged. (Non-native speaker, student of color, male)

Exploring the use of one's personal voice through a personal narrative was the goal of the first essay assignment, given during the second week of the quarter. The following is an excerpt from that assignment:

Gathering: *Essentially we started the gathering process for this paper with our first class when we asked you to begin thinking about the topics in this class such as identity, culture, stories, and communication. Asking you to read Peggy McIntosh's article, "Unpacking the Invisible Knapsack," and write about it was another step in gathering your own responses and ideas about issues of identity as they relate to privilege, class, race, gender, and sexual orientation. Allan Johnson* *is very clear about his focus in* Power, Privilege, and Difference *when he says, "For myself, it means I have to take the initiative to find out how privilege operates in the world, how it affects people, and what all that has to do with me. It means I have to think the unthinkable, speak the unspeakable, break the silence, acknowledge the elephant, and then take my share of responsibility for what comes next" (10–11). In our next book, David Mura* (Where Body Meets Memory) *will add a focus on his journey as a Japanese American man struggling with his race, identity, and sexuality. Our main purpose in this class and for this piece of writing will be to encourage you to find your "voice" as you explore something about yourself and your experiences that you can add to the conversation and help break the silence. To begin your paper, use your in-class response to McIntosh, look at your notes from the film,* The Color of Fear, *and from the lecture on "The Politics of Location" given by the Women's Studies professor, Karen Stuhldreher.*

Assignment for this narrative/personal essay: *Write a personal narrative about an experience that has shaped your identity, values, and/or understanding, specifically around the issues of race, ethnicity, gender, sexual orientation, and/or social class, AND reflect on how this experience has shaped your identity, values, and/or understanding. Some questions to consider might be: In this experience, were you in the position of having or not having privilege? What social institutions shaped your experience? What did you learn about your race, gender, sexual orientation, or social class identity? What changes, if any, did you make after this experience?*

Note: *The experience need not be a large life-defining moment; it can be something as simple as your first day at a new school. The important thing is that you reflect upon what you learned about your identity from the experience.*

Audience: *You should write thinking of our coordinated studies community as your audience. Don't write about something that is too private to share with anyone in this class. The papers should be able to be read publicly.*

How did students do with this initial foray into the discovery of their own voice and their reflection of their identity formation? The following are responses from students writing more than six weeks later, as the course was ending:

> Writing in the first person and including my own personal account has been a great but challenging process. I have found that in the past many of my instructors have deemed the word "I," if used in an essay, as a swear word, and have forbade its use. I also had not been taught much about brainstorming. When writing a personal account and having so many options, an answer is not really pointed out in the book. I had to really dig deep to find the answer. (White student, female)

> [I]t was hard for me to get started on an essay, but once I got started writing I could not stop. I never realized that I had so much to share about myself with other people. I learned that I don't like to speak because my writing speaks for the words that cannot come out of my mouth. I feel my writing is my voice. (Non-native speaker, student of color, male)

Like everything in the course which built on the knowledge and skills learned in the previous weeks, students' second paper (assigned in week seven) was an opportunity to practice an even more difficult writing challenge—a blending of creative storytelling with more structured analytical writing about the memoir or fiction we had read. Here is another excerpt from that assignment:

Focus on writing about and using literature: *As we finish reading* Dreaming in Cuban *and begin reading our last book,* Love Medicine *by Louise Erdrich, you should find common themes, interesting characters, and more fictional representations of how we search for our identity in culture and stories. We have seen how David Mura wrote about his own life and told us a non-linear story of his growth into adulthood as a Japanese American man. Even though the next three books are fiction, these writers each will admit that some of their own lives, families, and most certainly culture is represented in the stories they tell. They also include some of the myths that have become part of the culture and helped support an understanding of ourselves as members of a universal humanity who seeks to find meaning in our lives. Those of you who find these stories fascinating or difficult have the honor of entering another culture on the pages of these books. The authors are our teachers and we bring questions and desires of our own as we read these stories and connect them to our own lives.*

Paper topics: *For this second formal paper, we want you to combine using "writing about literature" with some story from your own life experience. The "personal" section of your essay could be the introduction or a paragraph or two in the middle or at the end after you have explored a theme or character from our books. You could use a short epigraph, a poem, or a story from your own family or an interview or conversation with someone in your family to bring the personal to your discussion of the literature. As we saw when Lee Mun Wah visited our class, the history of our name, our family, our dreams, all combine to make us who we are. Gloria Naylor did suffer emotionally, and she did move back and forth from the North to the South. Cristina Garcia could not have written* Dreaming in Cuban *without the historical reality of the Cuban revolution and the movement of her family between the United States and Cuba. Louise Erdrich writes* Love Medicine *and sets the story on and near the reservation that her family is from in North Dakota. She is Ojibwa-French and German-American like some of her characters.*

As we expected, many students found this second essay much more challenging than the first essay and struggled to find a way to weave personal experience with the themes from the books. But in the end, students found the experience worthwhile:

> Writing these essays helped me think about and process information and ideas in the readings, videos, guest presentations, and class discussions because I was forced, and allowed, to analyze myself in relation to all that I was learning. From their examples, I was shown how to tell the story of my own identity . . . In the end, I found a way to tie it all together; my truth, my analysis of what we were learning in the classroom, and my interpretations of the literature.
> (White student, female)

Sharing Cross-Cultural Stories

Our third step in intentionally creating a safe space was to deepen cross-cultural communication through the sharing of stories. Throughout the quarter, we heard many different kinds of cultural stories. Certainly the most obvious were the cultural stories of the authors we were reading. To encourage students to read these stories more thoughtfully and thoroughly we assigned weekly seminar papers.

The writing of these papers helped students practice and improve their critical reading, thinking, and writing skills:

> Writing the individual seminar papers allowed me to prepare well for the in-class seminar discussions. The papers helped me to truly process my thoughts about the various books, and to go deeper within myself to analyze the response to the things that I was reading. (White student, male)

A corollary practice we used to push students into more thoughtful reading was to ask them to examine the stories within their historical context. We did this by assigning weekly research assignments. For example, when we were reading David Mura's book, we asked students to spend one week researching and reporting on the Japanese American internment camp. When we were reading Christina Garcia's novel about the culture of Cuba, students researched different elements about the Cuban culture and about the history of the United States and Cuba since the Bay of Pigs. These mini-research assignments deepened students' understanding of the cultural complexity of these stories.

A second "chapter" of stories we encouraged were from the students themselves. Because the class was richly culturally diverse, we provided time each week for students to practice their listening skills while they heard each other's stories. We called this time "cultural conversations" and as one student writes:

> I have learned volumes from the stories we studied and just as much from the people in this class. For example, Rex (not his real name), who is in my seminar group, helped me understand more about his culture. He has given me an understanding about what it is like to be an immigrant from an African country and how the racism in this country has affected him. This is a perspective I could not have gotten anywhere else. I learned from Yin (not his real name) what it is like to be pulled over by a police officer for "driving while Asian," and yet he has a deep appreciation of the opportunity to be in this country and could be described by some as a patriot. Sue (not her real name) told me what it felt like to be the outsider and different when she traveled to Colombia to meet her husband's parents. (White student, female)

Our last "chapter" of cultural stories came from guest speakers. Mark Mitsui, NSCC's Director of Student Success and Retention, came twice to our class to share his knowledge about and his personal experience with the Japanese American internment camps. Mark has spent much of his life studying the impact of the camp experience on the Japanese American community. Because his father was interned, Mark's interest is both personal *and* scholarly. After describing the historical and (il)legal circumstances which resulted in the internment camps, Mark led students in an experiential exercise to foster deeper understanding of what it feels like to be treated as the "other." Students were given a few minutes to decide which of their possessions they would take, leave behind, and/or sell. Students were also asked, at the end of the exercise, to mark mock ballots in response to the two questions Japanese Americans were asked: "Do you swear allegiance to the United States?" and "Do you abdicate any loyalty to the Japanese Emperor?" This vote was in order to better understand the "No-No" Boy and "Yes-Yes" Boy division within the Japanese American community. As is traditionally the case in our classroom when the Japanese American internment camp experience is discussed, the majority of students were shocked to learn about this tragedy and then angry that they were never exposed to this historic truth in their high school history lessons.

We were equally fortunate to have Lee Mun Wah, producer of nationally known videos *The Color of Fear* and *Last Chance for Eden*, visit our class and share how racism ended his career as a teacher after his mother was murdered and forced him to feel the pain of that experience and search to find purpose from that tragedy. Both of these cultural storytellers created profound moments for us in the classroom to practice ways of listening and communicating more honestly and empathetically with each other. As one student wrote:

> Mun Wah was definitely one of the most influential figures for me in this class. It was through watching his films that I started to actually feel the affects of white racism on people of color. When he came to our class, I was overwhelmed by his presence, but more than that, I was overwhelmed by the way he was able to make me see what I was a part of. He made me see everyone in the class and become curious in a way that I hadn't been before. I felt like I would be losing the opportunity of a lifetime if I didn't take the time to learn more about the people I was sharing this experience with. I feel so blessed to have been able to meet so many different people in this class, to hear their perspectives, and to be able to talk so candidly about such sensitive topics. I feel so lucky that others have

> shared such personal parts of their life with me and I will never forget this class as long as I live. (Student of color, female)

In reflecting on the impact of this coordinated studies course on the lives of our students, we asked ourselves this question: Is the creation of a balanced learning environment, one that carefully and thoughtfully blends the "softer" human elements of nurture, personal voice, listening, and emotional honesty with the "harder" academic elements of critical thinking and writing, and a growing appreciation of a diverse world, a more effective long-range way of educating students to ultimately be "intensely interested in the development of each individual, of the group as a whole, and of a more democratic society" (Belenky, et al. 1999, 14)? Our students answer this question in these ways:

> It has been a long time since I was excited about school, but this class took my school interest to whole other level. I looked forward to coming; listening to people's stories and learning things about myself I never knew. I think about things differently. I hear a little better and sometimes the sounds scare and surprise me. It isn't all the time, but I feel like I sometimes see the world around me in a different light. I am more aware of the things usually left unsaid. There is so much left to be learned, and I hope this is only the beginning of my journey. (White student, female)

> This class has changed the way I look at life and the people in it. I want to meet new people and experience their cultures. If I had not taken this class I would just be one of those people who go on with their lives without knowing the richness that lies within each human being. (White student, male)

It seems to us that the intentional blending of the "soft" and "hard" elements of a learning community, coupled with a commitment to honesty, developing personal voice, and sharing stories across cultures, helps to develop a new way of being together—or as one student said so simply, "we have learned to speak in a language that human hearts, and not just minds, can understand."

Endnotes

1. The class consisted of 23 females, 18 males, 19 students of color, 22 white students, 13 non-native English speakers, with an average age of 30 years old.

References

Belenky, M. F., L. A. Bond, and J. S. Weinstock. 1999. *A Tradition That Has No Name: Nurturing the Development of People, Families, and Communities.* New York: Basic Books.

Erdrich, L. 1993. *Love Medicine.* New York: Perennial.

Garcia, C. 1993. *Dreaming in Cuban.* New York: Ballantine Books.

Gilligan, C. 1993. *In a Different Voice: Psychological Theory and Women's Development.* Cambridge, MA: Harvard University Press.

Johnson, A. 2001. *Privilege, Power, and Difference.* New York: McGraw Hill.

McIntosh, P. 1988. "White Privilege: Unpacking the Invisible Knapsack." Excerpted from Working Paper 189, *White Privilege and Male Privilege: A Personal Account of Coming to See Correspondences through Work in Women's Studies*. Wellesley Center for Women.

Mun Wah, L. 1997. *The Color of Fear*, VHS. Berkeley, CA: Stirfry Productions.

———. 2002. *Last Chance for Eden*, VHS. Berkeley, CA: Stirfry Productions.

Mura, D. 1997. *Where Body Meets Memory: An Odyssey of Race, Sexuality and Identity.* New York: Anchor Books.

Naylor, G. 1993. *Mama Day.* New York: Vintage Books.

Carol Hamilton is an English instructor at North Seattle Community College. Jane Lister Reis teaches communications at North Seattle Community College and helps to coordinate the learning community program.

Classroom Strategies for Learning Community Faculty: Situated Knowledge for Global Citizenship

Phyllis van Slyck

> *If we embrace the promise of diversity, of creative conflict . . . we still face one final fear—the fear that a live encounter with otherness will challenge or even compel us to change our lives. This is not paranoia: the world really is out to get us! Otherness, taken seriously, always invites transformation, calling us not only to new facts and theories and values but also to new ways of living our lives.*
>
> Parker J. Palmer, *The Courage to Teach*

LaGuardia Community College has one of the most diverse student populations of any community college in the United States, and its faculty have been designing and teaching in learning communities since 1976. LaGuardia also has a long-standing commitment to deepening faculty and student awareness of diversity issues. I will draw on this rich set of experiences to address the following questions, given a college with a diverse population and a range of academic preparedness, how do you help learning community faculty develop the skills necessary to be good teachers? What are the core skills and knowledge and how do you invite faculty to learn them?

Fortunately, for those of us teaching in learning communities at LaGuardia and for the college as a whole, the institutional commitment to diversity work, professional development, and creating purposeful occasions for reflection has always been strong. The college's commitment to expanding our learning community models, professional development, and dialogue about diversity and global citizenship is undergoing a renewal for a number of important reasons. First, in the spring of 2003, LaGuardia hired thirty-five new faculty, and we are in the process of hiring about forty more as part of a university-wide commitment to the City University New York (CUNY) community colleges (this means that by fall 2004, 25 percent to 30 percent of our faculty will be new). Second, in the fall of 2001, the LaGuardia Center for Teaching and Learning was initiated to support professional development programs already in place and to create new opportunities for reflection about teaching—and diversity—across the campus. Third, in response to student surveys that indicated a need for a greater sense of connection to the college and a more immediate immersion in the major, First Year Academies, which offer students one or more developmental courses, a course in their major and a first-year seminar dedicated to the major, were piloted in spring 2004. And, finally, as part of LaGuardia's strategic plan, and in response to an ongoing dialogue about diversity issues on campus, the president of the college, Dr. Gail Mellow, has initiated a task force on internationalization whose purpose is "to ensure that the structures and practices of the institution support an international educational experience for all students."

In what follows, I focus on the requisite knowledge and skills for learning community practitioners working with diverse students whose academic preparation is uneven. I will share some recent faculty dialogue and professional development work on diversity, including the self-critique we try to engage in, and what we consider to be "best practices." I will then develop these general ideas by offering some case studies of this work—in practice—in our learning communities.

Some Background

Located in Long Island City, Queens, one of the most culturally diverse boroughs in the United States, LaGuardia Community College opened its doors in 1971 to 500 students. Of our 12,000 matriculated students today, 65 percent are foreign born and 49 percent have been in thc United States less than five years. Our students come from 160 countries and speak 116 languages. This means that a very high percentage of incoming students must complete ESL courses before beginning courses in their major. Faculty teaching introductory courses and also core courses in the major must continue to address second language issues. In addition, the majority of LaGuardia students need at least one developmental course (English, reading, or math). In terms of external issues relevant to student success, while 38 percent of our entering students are recent high school graduates, 47 percent have been working for some time and 63 percent will continue to work more than twenty hours a week. These students' financial responsibilities are very different from the traditional full-time college student in the United States: 19 percent have children; two thirds of these children are under six years of age, and some students help support families outside the country. In incoming surveys students say that their greatest concern is being able to keep up with their studies, given financial difficulties, family responsibilities, and lack of academic preparation. Many stop out for a semester to earn the money to continue, and it takes five to seven years for the average student to complete a two-year associate degree. In spite of numerous obstacles LaGuardia students have big dreams: 85 percent plan to continue their education.[1]

For LaGuardia faculty, learning communities and diversity practice have always been deeply connected. Our first learning communities, the liberal arts "freedom clusters," were faculty designed and initiated in the mid-1970s. Today LaGuardia has a variety of integrated learning community programs. Entering liberal arts and science majors choose from a menu of six to eight clusters. All clusters are organized around a theme and all have four courses from the core liberal arts and science curriculum (introductory courses in music, philosophy, theatre, journalism, film, sociology, psychology, biology, biochemistry, anatomy, and physiology), along with an English composition course, a research paper course, and an integrated seminar hour that is team-taught. Topics for the research paper course are interdisciplinary and based on materials in all the other courses. Current cluster titles give an indication of the diversity of themes and courses offered: *Reefer Madness: A Philosophical Inquiry into Drugs and Society*; *Truth, Lies and Videotape*; *Names, Labels and Stereotypes*; *I Am What I Am: Identity, Performance and Poetic Justice*; *Fighting for Our Rights*; *Women and Society; The Sociology and Culture of the Family*; *Exploring the City Through Music, Literature, and Theatre*; *From Movies to the Internet*; *Harlem on My Mind: The Harlem Renaissance*; and *Science: Beauty or Beast?*

A developmental cluster, the New Student House, was initiated by faculty in 1991 to create a learning community for LaGuardia's most at-risk students, those who needed basic skills courses in reading, writing, and speech. Today the House offers basic reading, basic writing along with a college-level content course, and a Freshman Seminar. In the 1990s, faculty in LaGuardia's ESL credit program began offering an ESL version of the New Student House and a variety of ESL courses paired with college-level content courses throughout the curriculum. Approximately twenty-five such pairs are offered each semester: ESL courses are paired with sociology, human services, computing, accounting and business, humanities, and reading. Institutional data indicates that ESL students who take college-level courses paired with ESL courses are outperforming students taking the same courses independently, even though the latter are, technically, two courses "above" them.

In response to student frustration about being able to take courses in their major, LaGuardia piloted *First Year Academies*, which in spring 2004 offered entering students one or more developmental courses with a course in their major. It is hoped that all first-year students who need at least one basic skills course will enter one of four academies: business, technology, liberal arts, or natural and applied sciences. In each academy, the basic skills course and the first-year seminar are focused on the major, as well as additional activities on campus such as orientation events, career workshops, study skills workshops, and virtual interest groups. LaGuardia's learning communities reflect a truly integrated practice: each is organized around a theme and faculty plan, refine, and evaluate their curriculum and pedagogy.[2]

Faculty Dialogue and Professional Development

> *It is important to go beyond the 'nod': we need to do more than acknowledge diversity.*
>
> Paula Nesoff, LaGuardia Faculty

Hand in hand with diversity work in learning communities, the college as a whole has been engaged in discussions about diversity and pluralism in the classroom for much of the last three decades. A task force initiated in the late 1980s worked to infuse pluralism throughout the curriculum and continues to offer a variety of seminars on diversity issues. Annual opening sessions for faculty and regular instructional staff meetings have been devoted—in whole or in part—to diversity issues. The Center for Teaching and Learning invites faculty and staff from across the college to present at weekly brown bag lunches on pedagogical and diversity issues. LaGuardia's Declaration of Pluralism, which is a part of the college catalogue and is used by faculty as a teaching tool in both learning communities and stand-alone courses, sums up the spirit of this work. (See Figure 1)

In response to the question, "What do we mean by diversity at LaGuardia?" faculty at an Instructional Staff Meeting held in fall 2001, volunteered many aspects of diversity in addition to nationality, language, ethnicity, and gender, including educational background, level of acculturation, age, sexual orientation, disability, traumatic background, ideological beliefs, maturity, religious background, economic status, citizenship status, health, learning styles, and attitudes about diversity. The ensuing discussion (How does diversity affect your teaching and what issues would you like to explore further with

Figure 1

Declaration of Pluralism: LaGuardia Community College

We are a diverse community at LaGuardia Community College.
We strive to become a pluralistic community.
We respect diversity as reflected in such areas as race, culture, ethnicity, gender, religion, age, sexual orientation, disability and social class.

As a pluralistic community we will:
* Celebrate: individual and group diversity.
* Honor: the rights of people to speak and be heard on behalf of pluralism.
* Promote: intergroup cooperation, understanding and communication.
* Acknowledge: each others' contributions to the community.
* Share: beliefs, customs and experiences which enlighten us about members of our community.
* Affirm: each others' dignity.
* Seek: further ways to learn about and appreciate one another.
* Confront: the expression of de-humanizing stereotypes, incidents where individuals or groups are excluded because of difference, the intolerance of diversity and the forces of racism, sexism, heterosexism, homophobia, disability discrimination, ageism, classism and ethnocentrism that fragment the community into antagonistic individuals and groups.

We believe by carrying out these actions we, as students, faculty and staff can achieve social change and the development of a society in which each individual can achieve her or his maximum potential.

colleagues?) also revealed that LaGuardia faculty, despite an awareness of the complexity of diversity, see the need for a deeper investigation of how to create a truly pluralistic community. Observations about what was still needed at an institution that takes diversity work seriously included:

• acknowledgement of faculty diversity issues: how can practices be improved; how can we be more sensitive to diversity issues among our peers

• awareness of our teaching styles in relation to student learning styles; knowledge and flexibility required; sharing of ideas about inclusive pedagogy
• recognition not only of diversity but cross-cultural commonalities
• recognition of different student expectations about classroom, teaching, and education
• value of diverse student experience at LaGuardia, but sensitivity (spokesperson issue)
• going beyond the nod: doing more than acknowledging diversity; ideas for dialogue; deeper investigation of pluralism
• reflections on how faculty position themselves in global classroom (openness, vigilance towards our own assumptions)
• think globally and bring a deeper knowledge about other cultures into our classrooms
• texts with explicit awareness of diverse examples, perspectives
• dealing with homophobia as the last "acceptable" prejudice
• reflections on ways diversity is an advantage at LaGuardia—for faculty and students—ways we do bridge cultures; time for reflection on difficulties and common experiences needed

It is important to note that this meeting took place directly after 9/11, and our college came together, purposefully, to connect our work on diversity to this tragic event. We realized we needed to go beyond places of comfort and to engage in difficult dialogues. Faculty noted that diversity issues among faculty were sometimes not acknowledged or understood, that faculty needed to be reflective about self-positioning, and that strategies for hiring and retaining diverse faculty needed to be improved. We agreed that recognizing diverse student expectations about education, teachers, and the classroom was important; that faculty should strive to be more aware of teaching styles in relation to student learning styles, and that a deeper infusion of global cultural issues into our teaching practice was needed. Finally, faculty indicated that commonalities as well as differences should be emphasized and explored, and that we should be reflecting on ways faculty and students at LaGuardia *do* bridge cultures and recognize and respect difference.

To show how our professional development workshops help faculty integrate theory and practice, I would like to describe two recent faculty seminars. At seminars, supported by the LaGuardia Center for Teaching and Learning, faculty received either course release or a stipend for their participation. Faculty involved were not exclusively participants in learning communities, but individual workshops and discussions within these seminars were devoted to learning community issues.

During the 2002–03 academic year, a group of eleven faculty participated in a Teaching Portfolio Seminar. The group consisted of both junior and senior faculty, and five members of the group were veteran learning community practitioners. This seminar was collaboratively designed and led by faculty. Our goal was to reflect on our teaching and to create online portfolios to share with our community. We were inspired, in part, by a student electronic portfolio project currently underway at LaGuardia. These teaching portfolios were not related in any way to our tenure and promotion process; they were designed to engage in reflective practice—to discuss the challenges we face and share effective strategies to address those challenges. We created several categories for our work, including "Community and Collaboration," "Diversity," and "Reflective Practice," and we designed reflection questions and student activities for each section.[3]

We articulated particular questions to consider in the "Diversity" section of our portfolios, including the following: How do specific cultural and social aspects of your identity influence your teaching? How important is it to consider issues of diversity in your curriculum design? How do you integrate issues of diversity into your curriculum? Describe some challenges and/or problems you have faced teaching in an institution with such a diverse student population. In addition, everyone was asked to describe a classroom practice that recognizes student diversity.

In their final evaluations, faculty were asked how the Seminar helped them in their teaching and, more generally, in their 'lives' at LaGuardia. They spoke of the importance of "frank, open discussions" and a "safe space" for dialogue, and many indicated that the emphasis on reflection—in classroom assignments and for faculty themselves—was most valuable. One faculty member said, "The written contributions helped me to discover what I thought about my teaching." Another wrote that the seminar offered her an opportunity to think about what she wanted to change in her teaching, and that she reshaped activities in light of our readings and discussions. In response to the question, "What have you changed in your teaching as a result of the seminar?" several noted that they were incorporating more opportunities for reflective assignments and activities related to diversity issues. Our reading and discussion of Parker Palmer's *The Courage to Teach* and Steven D. Brookfield's *Becoming a Critically*

Reflective Teacher were the foundation for lively discussion and offered concrete strategies—especially for reflective practice.[4]

A second example of the kind of professional development LaGuardia is currently engaged in involves the orientation and support of new faculty. This is our primary opportunity to introduce new faculty to our diverse students and their needs, to our learning communities, and to core practices we value in learning communities and beyond. In fall 2003 we welcomed thirty new faculty to LaGuardia, and a year-long seminar for this group was initiated, consisting of a two-day orientation, a winter one-day institute, and monthly workshops throughout the academic year. In the orientation institute for this New Faculty Colloquium, we asked new faculty to reflect on what resources they bring and what skills they would like to develop in response to a description of LaGuardia students (based on a variety of information from the institutional profile on students' essays). Responses gathered from this exercise became the basis for future workshops.

Since effective design and assessment apply not only to students in learning communities but to faculty as well, LaGuardia faculty are introduced to self-assessment models such as Stephen D. Brookfield's reflective teaching journals. Drawing on articles and workshop materials familiar to learning community practitioners including Peter T. Ewell's "Organizing for Learning" and Grant Wiggins and Jay McTighe's "Backward Design for Curricular Integration," we introduced new faculty to some of the foundations of learning community practice. Ewell reminds us that institutions need an "alternative design vision that starts with students and what they need to be successful as learners." Towards that end, we invite faculty to design learner-centered activities for the classroom, try them out, and create assessment occasions to evaluate their assignments. The faculty seminar itself models these learning practices as faculty collaboratively develop their activities and share concerns, and as seminar leaders assess the workshops. The core practices we have highlighted in our workshops for all new faculty—community and collaboration, active learning, reflective practice, and diversity practice—match those described in depth in *Learning Communities: Reforming Undergraduate Education* by Smith, et al. (2004).

To show how these general ideas about diversity and learning community practice are realized at LaGuardia, I will examine two learning communities—a liberal arts cluster and a capstone liberal arts seminar—where students return to a meta-learning community at the end of their careers at LaGuardia. Here they reflect on how their learning in core liberal arts courses has shaped their understanding of global citizenship.

Lessons from the Learning Community Classroom

The decentering of authority through seminar work, collaborative learning, and active learning, a hallmark of learning community pedagogy, promotes shared responsibility for learning and, when properly shaped through collaborative ground rules, a responsible analysis of complex issues. In addition, the integrated curriculum of learning communities promotes a deeper understanding of different perspectives—and of the individual's responsibility to grapple with them. Learning community faculty not only work on curriculum together; they use pedagogies that acknowledge and honor diverse learning styles. Robert Ibarra's description of minority students as "high context learners" is repeatedly confirmed in the LaGuardia learning community classroom. Group projects and problem-based learning activities offered by faculty help students who have not had a successful educational experience in high school to develop analytic skills and cross-disciplinary understanding as well as social skills. Many of our learning community faculty are also very familiar with the benefits of classroom assessment techniques and use them as a way of identifying pedagogies that promote intellectual and emotional growth. One-minute paper responses to identify the "muddiest point" and longer reflective journals are assigned—often with questions designed to address meta-cognition (how has your thinking about this issue changed?)—as well as end-of-term assessments of the entire learning community program. Some questions might include, "How did the cluster themes relate to one another in all of the courses, for example through written assignments, discussion, field activities?" or "The purpose of the Integrated Seminar is to help you make connections among the disciplines. How did the seminar do this for you?"

Case Study #1
Integrated Learning in a Liberal Arts Cluster

In a liberal arts cluster offered fall of 2003, faculty in English, theatre, and philosophy constructed a joint syllabus where a set of key questions could be effectively examined in the three disciplines and compared across disciplines, throughout the semester.[5]

Key Questions for Liberal Arts Cluster

In this cluster, I Am What I Am: Identity, Performance, and Poetic Justice, *we will examine and debate fundamental questions about the nature of human identity. How can we characterize human nature? Is human nature inherently selfish? Are we determined to be what we are or are we free to create ourselves? How does society control the shape our identities take? In what ways are we not free to define ourselves? How do we know the "truth" about another person or even about ourselves? Is memory accurate? What assumptions do we make about others? What are these assumptions based on? To what extent do we construct, change, and perform our identities and is this a kind of "truth"?*

These introductory questions are used in a team-taught brainstorming session on the first or second day of class, and since answers to these broad questions take a semester, or a lifetime, to develop, the questions evolve into themes and issues related to readings and other activities throughout the course. The English and theatre professors agreed on four plays to be studied *(Oedipus Rex*, *Fences*, *Death and the Maiden*, and *M Butterfly*), and the three faculty chose several films that would complement the plays and address issues of identity in more complex ways. These included *Roshomon*, *Memento*, *Boys Don't Cry*, *The Laramie Project*, and the HBO film, *Normal*.

Many learning community faculty stress the importance of creating a foundation of openness and trust early in the semester. Only within this framework, often supported by collaboratively designed ground rules, will students feel safe sharing who they are. An early in-class online writing assignment asked students to respond to a series of questions about their identity. The online format made it possible for students to view and respond to each other's postings. Students were asked to respond to any two questions.

First Questions: Reflective In-Class Writing
(to be followed by group discussion and reflective writing)

1. What individuals have been most influential in shaping your identity?

2. What social institutions have been most influential?

3. Can you think of a powerful defining moment or an incident that shaped your identity in some meaningful way (good or bad)?

4. Can you think of a time you struggled against a definition being imposed on you?

5. Are there times when you are aware of performing an identity that is not truly you? Is this necessarily bad? Why do we do this?

6. In what ways do you feel that you are free to change your identity or nature? In what ways do you feel change is impossible?

7. Why is it important to believe you can change? What are the ethical implications of believing your identity is in process, not fixed?

The online writing assignment was given by the English professor, but with the students' permission, the theatre and philosophy faculty were "enrolled" in the course so that they could read the students' postings. This gives all members of the faculty team a common knowledge of the students as well as an awareness of the skills they bring to their writing and thinking. It was immediately apparent that the answers to these questions were "typical" of LaGuardia students in their diversity and poignancy. For a powerful moment or incident that shaped your identity, one student wrote about being imprisoned and educating himself; another wrote about being placed in a homeless shelter for the mentally disturbed by her parents who disapproved of her interracial relationship. A third described the arrest of his brother, the shooting and death of a friend, and his decision not to follow the path of selling drugs. As students responded to each other's stories, bonds began to develop and at the end of the semester, when asked to write about the learning community experience, many spoke of the importance of the personal revelations shared in our early classes. Against some traumatic personal experiences, questions of freedom and determinism were debated in philosophy and examined in relation to *Oedipus Rex* and August Wilson's *Fences*. Questions of ethics, personal responsibility, and justice initiated in our discussion of *Oedipus Rex* were debated in a contemporary context in *Death and the Maiden*, Ariel Dorfman's powerful depiction of the consequences of the Pinochet regime.

Perhaps the most complex and important segment of the cluster was the discussion that centered around questions of gender and identity, initiated by a critical analysis of David Henry Hwang's *M Butterfly* followed by screenings of *Boys Don't Cry*, *The Laramie Project*, and *Normal* and an interview with a transgender faculty member. What follows are two student responses that make explicit some of the intellectual and emotional growth that emerges through an acknowledged confrontation with values and a recognition of the way these values are socially constructed.

> The film *Boys Don't Cry* helped me step aside and really see how society has molded us to become blind savages towards gays, bisexuals, cross dressers, etc. I was always told that the people that slept with their own kind were never forgiven for that sin. As a young child, I couldn't imagine how God could forgive the worst serial killer, just by him/her repenting, but he wouldn't forgive a person that had a natural attraction to his or her own kind. I never questioned it because I knew that I would never be answered; it was just the way it was. I never tried to interact with them because of the fear of never being accepted or forgiven by God. Now I am much older and thankfully, open-minded. I can finally stand up and say what I feel and why I feel that way. I now can cut my thread from the needle that has always sewn me to a certain patch.
> (Annette Gomez, student)

> Matthew *(The Laramie Project)* and Tina *(Boys Don't Cry)* were just expressing themselves in a way they thought they were comfortable. But we could not see their comfort; we could only see our comfort, and for us to be in a zone of comfort we must take them into a zone of discomfort. Tina and Matthew can both be considered modern day martyrs. They both died because of their beliefs. I believe that they were trying to find their identity, but, because of society, we ended their search early. I truly think that these two movies really changed my life. I am accepting a homosexual as just another person, another person that sheds tears just like me. This goes for everyone, from people of a different race, ethnic group, and even financial standing. I see them as another person who bleeds like me. They breathe, eat, sleep, and do almost everything like me. So why shouldn't I treat them the way I would like to be treated? (Jaime Stone, student)

For learning community veterans, these responses are powerful evidence of what William Perry describes as the integration of knowledge learned from others with personal experience and reflection.[6] Annette's description of "cutting the thread" is a powerful metaphor for what can happen in a learning community when new ideas and perspectives challenge what students have been taught. And Jaime poignantly describes the way others interfere with our search for ourselves. Unwittingly echoing Shakespeare's Shylock ("does not a Jew bleed . . ."), Jaime, like Annette, describes and reflects on his own transformation.

Dialogue among faculty teaching in learning communities is an exhilarating blend of enthusiasm, creativity, and troubleshooting as we assess the progress of our students, refine connections among our disciplines, and look for learner-centered approaches to ongoing projects. We share the results of our most successful assignments (the philosophy professor's Socratic dialogue assignment, the theatre professor's identity improvisation assignment), and we marvel at the connections students make on their own (applying Plato's *Symposium on Love* to *Boys Don't Cry*; finding a connection between "blindness" in *Oedipus Rex* and *The Laramie Project*). We also touch base concerning those students who are having the most difficulty or who are not completing their work. Sometimes we make exceptions as we strive to support every student in the way he or she needs, but, overall, faculty feel it is worth it if we succeed in retaining and encouraging those students who are often anonymous failures in large public institutions. What we hope for, and sometimes observe, during the semester as we ask students to evaluate their experience, is that the core values we as faculty associate with learning communities have been incorporated into our students'approach to learning, and that at the end of the semester they feel confident of their ability to construct their own meaning.

Case study #2
Reflective Growth in a Meta-Learning Community: Capstone Seminar on Humanism, Science, and Technology

The capstone seminar at LaGuardia invites graduating liberal arts students to engage in the kind of dialogue and reflection that were characteristic of their beginning experience in the liberal arts cluster. They are asked to reflect on knowledge and perspective gained in liberal arts core courses by applying this knowledge to significant problems and struggles of the twenty-first century—situations where humanistic concerns are sometimes at odds with advances in science and technology. Faculty teach this seminar in highly individual ways, focusing on an individual theme such as disease over the centuries, or a particular part of the world, such as the experience of colonialism in Latin America.

Students in capstone liberal arts seminars are regularly asked to reflect on the way the learning community has changed their way of thinking. What follows is an example of a final essay Max Rodriguez of the Humanities Department offers his students. He purposefully asks students to reflect on their own growth as thinkers.

Reflection is a deliberate attempt to reveal yourself as a learner to yourself and to others, to question critically your learning style, and to give examples that document your learning in a course or set of courses. The main goal of reflection is to think critically about your learning experience and to encourage connections between a body of knowledge and your own learning style.

1. Select a writing assignment that in your opinion demonstrates what you have learned in this course.

2. Write a short essay giving examples from your own writing to illustrate your points.

3. Use some or all of the questions below to stir your thoughts:

- Describe why you chose this item for your reflection.

- What new knowledge and skills did you acquire through the content and activities of this course?

- Explain how the writing you chose is a good example of your skills as a writer and thinker.

- What connections have you made between this course and other courses you have take before, work and/or personal experiences? Give details.

4. Discuss briefly how you feel about reflecting on your own learning. A paragraph will suffice.

Student responses reveal an ability to transfer a paradigm from one context to another, often one that has personal relevance to the writer. Responses also reflect layered reflection about social history and power relations embedded in certain practices:

> At the beginning of this course all I knew about Plato was that he was an old, smart, dead Greek philosopher. As we discussed *The Allegory of the Cave* in more detail my ideas developed and changed. I realized that Plato's cave wasn't particularly thought provoking because of its story; it was the concept behind it that was. I was able to see examples of Plato's idea in history. The example of Plato's idea that I was best able to identify was with Malcolm X and his story. Like the men in Plato's cave, Malcolm and his friends believed in the "shadows." They were ignorant and uneducated to ways outside of the life they knew, which was a life of selling drugs

> and violence. However, as Malcolm left the cave (Harlem) and went to prison, he effectively distanced himself from his peers and became educated alone. He progressed and learned while his peers didn't. And when he returned to Harlem to enlighten them to the things he had learned, they ignored him. (Craig Daley, student)

What are the lessons learned by faculty at LaGuardia as they reflect on the relationship between diversity practice and learning communities? Under the category of "challenges," our faculty dialogue reveals that we recognize that diversity work is never done, that it requires constant rethinking, adjustment, sensitivity, and openness—effectively the same qualities that are needed for learning community work and for good teaching in general. Members of our 2002–03 Teaching Portfolio Seminar said that what was most needed and most difficult to find was reflective time to share strategies and concerns. LaGuardia faculty teach on average four courses per semester and contribute substantially to departmental activities and college-wide service. Finding time to assess their individual teaching as well as their work together in learning communities is often difficult. The Division of Academic Affairs and the LaGuardia Center for Teaching and Learning are committed to supporting professional development by offering some released time, but much of this work is grant funded and therefore difficult to guarantee as a permanent part of our culture. Currently, however, we are feeling very fortunate to be able to offer six yearlong professional development seminars in which diversity, active learning, and reflective practice are emphasized.

In the category of "best practices," learning community faculty would probably agree that building a safe space for community and time for reflection is as important for students as it is for faculty. Pedagogical materials presented here and on the Teaching Portfolio website suggest that collaborative, active learning assignments and projects specifically focused on diversity themes and issues are central to learning community curricula. Many of these activities show an intentional foregrounding of issues central to LaGuardia students such as immigration, hybridity, language difficulties, and empathy.

In a *Women and Society* cluster, Lorraine Cohen invites students to "look at gender oppression through the multiple lenses of women in this country and in other parts of the world. Important to this is an interview assignment that leads to a paper about a woman of an older generation, often the mother of the student. Since so many of the students' parents are immigrants and many of them are from working-class backgrounds, students have an opportunity to focus on the interplay between gender, class, and culture." Gail Green-Anderson, a veteran of many learning communities, uses an assignment related to Gabriel García Márquez's novella *Chronicle of a Death Foretold* as a way of inviting students to think about their own experience of translation: "I ask students, before they read the novella, to write a short autobiographical essay based on an experience with translation. Students wrote about translating from one language to another; those who spoke only English had the opportunity to write about an expression or joke that did not 'travel' from one social context to another. As we discussed *Chronicle of a Death Foretold*, we talked about issues related to translation. In this way, we recognized the power of language, not just *a* language, English. Since English is not the first language of most students in my class, this approach made students feel more confident and even proud of their expressive abilities in their first, second, or third languages."

If we look more deeply into classrooms where learning community work is taking place, the notion of holding back, of becoming the "guide on the side," emerges again and again. It becomes part of a reflective self-critique for many of us: "I was going to say something but . . . I waited"; or "I said something and wished I hadn't but the students solved the problem anyway." We can relate, in other words, to Parker Palmer's description of his struggle not to do the work for his students:

> [W]hen a student says something utterly untrue—everything in me wants to rise up and smite this falsehood with the Sword of Truth. If I want to encourage the conversation that the community of truth requires, I must learn to ask myself in that crucial instant a simple but demanding question: How quickly do I need to do the smiting? Can it wait thirty seconds? A minute? To the end of the hour? Until the next class? (1998, 134)

Here is faculty member Leonard Vogt's description of his struggle with a cluster discussion that got out of hand:

> In my liberal arts clusters, I teach around the themes of ethnicity, class, gender, and race, using Virginia Cyrus's *Experiencing Race, Class, and Gender in the U.S.* I assign around ten articles for each of the four themes and have students work in small groups to do reports on each of the articles. Recently, when reporting on the gender theme, one

> group was discussing an article called "Rape and Sexual Assault." The article's point was that rape has more to do with power than with sex but as the students made their report, the topic of women bringing on rape through what they wear or don't wear began to consume the conversation. I finally stopped the discussion, saying that the class was out of hand, that they were dealing with the topic far more from the emotions than the intellect and that this type of Jerry Springer approach to critical thinking was simply not appropriate or acceptable in a college classroom. One student asked if they could have five more minutes on the discussion since she thought what we were doing was very important. At that point a student who had not yet had a chance to report on her part of the article said: "The article ends by saying that nuns and women completely covered and even small children were sometimes raped; therefore what is worn or not worn is irrelevant to the cause of the action." That one student got the discussion back on course. The point of all this is that students often end up being the ones who really teach the class, if we trust them enough and even allow them to do what they have to do in their learning process.

While we would like to take credit for the purposeful structuring of activities and projects, as Vogt shows, the truth is that in learning communities we often observe the ways students take charge of their own knowledge. Our task, then, becomes to heighten their awareness of this process.

What is most meaningful to many faculty, despite our large classes, busy schedules, and impossible dreams, is our students' ability to apply what they are learning to new contexts, to look reflectively at ways they have changed, and their explicit valuing of insights and growth that have occurred during the cluster or seminar. It is the way students describe the transformative effects of being part of this kind of community:

> I think this cluster has helped us find our true selves because I've seen people changing; I can tell the difference from the beginning of the semester up to this point. We're all growing and we're acquiring knowledge from all of our classes that are applicable to our lives. I love the fact that there is so much potential in our class, that everybody has their own artist and philosopher inside, and it is also great to see the diversity of

ethnicity in our cluster; I love my cluster, I love my classmates and I thank my professors for all the help, patience and understanding they've offered us throughout the semester. (Joanna Ramirez, student)

Endnotes

1. Source: Office of Institutional Research, Institutional Profile (http://www.lagcc.cuny.edu/facts/default.aspx).
2. For more details about each of these learning community programs at LaGuardia, see our website: http://www.lagcc.cuny.edu/lc.
3. The website our Teaching Portfolios is at: http://www.lagcc.cuny.edu/tps.
4. Our teaching portfolio seminar were developed in dialogue with Judith Kamber, Director of the Center for Teaching and Learning at Northern Essex Community College, where she leads a faculty seminar called "Teaching in Community."
5. William J. Koolsbergen (theatre), Sonja Tanner (philosophy), and Phyllis van Slyck (English) taught this learning community.
6. See the LaGuardia Center for Teaching and Learning website for a description of these seminars: http://faculty.lagcc.cuny.edu/CTL/home.htm.

References

Brookfield, S. D. 1995. *Becoming a Critically Reflective Teacher*. San Francisco: Jossey Bass.

Ewell, P. 1997. "Creating a Learning College for the 21st Century: Organizing for Learning." *AAHE Bulletin*.

Ibarra, R. 2001. *Beyond Affirmative Action*. Madison, WI: The University of Wisconsin Press.

Palmer, P. J. 1998. *The Courage to Teach*. San Francisco: Jossey-Bass.

Perry, W. G. 1970. *Forms of Intellectual Development in the College Years: A Scheme*. New York: Holt, Rhinehart, Winston.

Smith, B., J. MacGregor, R. Matthews, and F. Gabelnick. 2004. *Learning Communities: Reforming Undergraduate Education*. San Francisco: Jossey-Bass.

Wiggins, G., and J. McTighe. 1998. "Backward Design for Curricular Integration." Chap. 1 in *Understanding by Design*. Alexandria, VA: Association for Supervision & Curriculum Development.

Phyllis van Slyck is an English professor at LaGuardia Community College.

Visible Border Crossers: Reflections on Faculty Collaboration

Debora Barrera Pontillo and Catherine Crain

Sometimes our teaching experiences change us in unforgettable ways. In fall 2002, we taught a learning community, *Education for Social Justice*, that combined an education course and a sociology course. Forty-six students enrolled. We had high hopes but the journey was much harder than we had anticipated. We would like to begin by sharing two letters that we wrote to each other shortly after the class was over. Then we describe our learning community in more detail, and how and why the class changed hearts—our students and our own. Perhaps it is no coincidence that our students' hearts were changed precisely because we had the courage to engage our own hearts in the process.

Our Letters: What We Learned

Dear Debora,

It was such an honor and privilege to teach with you. I learned so much—so much about you and your personal geography and so much about my own. We worked, struggled, laughed, and cried together and when all is said and done, I feel we are much closer and a much more powerful team on our campus.

Here is the geography of my experience last quarter. We planned the class together, combining classes we had taught before: my piece was Education 105: Introduction to Education, *and your piece was* Sociology 150: Multicultural Communication. *Together the learning community became* Education for Social Justice. *Our planning for the class went very smoothly—we worked well together and picked readings and assignments from our repertoire of previous experience. We also created some new things—our final project, for example, was a new creation, coming from a synergy of ideas we had each used before—asking the students to work at a community partnership site, keep a journal, do a research project (in teams) on a social justice issue coming out of their site work, develop a social action project (in teams), and document and reflect on these experiences.*

As the quarter started, I was impressed by your use of "Theatre of the Oppressed" activities and we used these each week to get students on their feet, moving and engaging in physical representations of some of the issues that our classwork raised. I was also impressed by your presence in the classroom—you are a powerful person and bring so much of yourself to your teaching. Slowly but surely, we moved from "comfortable" to "uncomfortable" territory for many of the students, and I'll admit, for me as well. We began to discuss issues of racism, classism, sexism—not from an historical perspective, but from a perspective of how power and privilege play out in the world we currently inhabit. You and I worked as a powerful team: you as a woman of color, I as an ally but someone who has rarely been a victim of oppression, walking with privilege most of my life.

We began to notice ways that power and privilege were sometimes obstacles in our own work as co-teachers. For example, students who were not comfortable approaching or confronting you would only visit me during office hours, perhaps hoping for a sympathetic ear as they were challenged to confront their own power and privilege. You and I spoke of this but it was hard for me to see or hear—nevertheless, I respected you and your perception and we began holding office hours together most days to interrupt these patterns.

I also noticed that we had different ways of teaching about issues of diversity. Given that I am not a person of color, most of my teaching about issues of diversity and education is not based in personal experience, but rather in what I have learned from books, videos, and observations. Our passions and interests overlapped to a great extent, but we had different lenses on the issues. I would often bring in a video, or give a mini-lecture with charts and graphs, for example, showing drop-out rates of students of color. You would then add your perspective to my presentations, providing first-person accounts to help students understand the emotional experience of oppression. Sometimes, I felt that my contributions were rather dry and sterile in comparison to the "real life" lens that you provided.

Our styles of communication and working were also different, more so than I had expected, given that we've worked as colleagues for three years. I tended to come to class with a fairly strict plan of what we would do and I found you to be more spontaneous—willing to modify the plan to respond to the energy of the moment and the needs of the students. There were days when I was uncomfortable, feeling that my contribution was pushed to the side, and I began to chafe internally. We spoke of this a few times, but it was a sore subject and our conversations often led to hurt feelings and misunderstandings. We also had different systems of grading and were trying to merge our two approaches. One day I gave you some instructions and I came across as patronizing. You told me that I was treating you as if you didn't have a brain in your head and I began to cry. We hugged and talked for a long time and I tried to reflect on how I was communicating with you. I interrogated myself about whether I was judging you as not being as "organized" as I was.

About halfway through the quarter, I remember feeling very tense and somewhat jealous about the way students responded to you with amazing love and respect—you command attention in a way that I never will—and it occurred to me how much I have to learn from you. I decided to stop struggling for control, and instead to relax and enjoy being in the space with you and the students. I tried to follow your lead and respond to the students instead of bringing in a rigid plan for the day. Our communication improved and we were able to speak honestly to each other about how we felt. We still had our struggles from time to time, but the energy had shifted and we were much more in tune with each other.

In a way, our struggles matched what was going on with our students. Although we were not completely open about the challenges we faced working together, or our different life experiences and cultural styles, we shared some of this with students. The class changed. Early on we had been met with a great deal of resistance, but mid-way through the quarter, the energy shifted for many students. Most became engaged and seemed to be changing their perspectives in some very deep ways. I feel fortunate to have been a witness to this and to have shared in the experience. There were days in class where students cried at the injustices they were seeing in their off-campus work. Students were beginning to care about social justice; their lives were changing.

The last day of class, we sat in a circle and each of us spoke about what the class had meant to us. I was moved to tears by the fact that some of the students who initially carried a façade of being callow, hard-hearted, and resistant to the messages of our class broke down and cried about how our class had changed their lives. I have never, in all my years of teaching, felt so good about what happened in a class. And I think that our struggles played a substantial role in enabling students to engage in a similar struggle.

Thank you Debora, for staying the course with me—for pushing and challenging me, for giving me the space to do the work I needed and wanted to do, and for your amazing unconditional love and forgiveness. What I take away:

- a much deeper understanding of power and privilege and how it

plays out in my life and the lives around me;
- a much deeper understanding that when we plan learning communities, we need to have a clear vision of the different lenses we bring—it is not enough to divide up the content. We may address the same content but bring different ways of knowing to that content. I need to interrogate myself carefully to make sure I don't subtly suggest that one way of knowing is superior to another;
- a much deeper understanding of some of my own control issues and how they can get in my way when working closely with others;
- a much deeper understanding of transformative educational experiences and how serendipitous and ephemeral they can be. I learned to stay open to possibilities and to chance happenings; and
- a fundamental re-affirming of my own belief in the power of love and keeping an open heart. We never gave up. Even when we were hurting and angry, we continued to engage with one another and to believe in the possibility of successfully negotiating these border crossings.

~ Catherine

* * *

Dear Catherine,

"Today we say enough; no longer will we live on bended knees."
Zapatistas, postcard from Chiapas, Mexico

how can i speak to this experience...to the boundaries, to the barriers, to the border lands...disrupting, contesting...how can you teach with me in a way that does not replicate colonial relationships? how can i teach with you and not blame you and mark you white? how does one teach one's lived experience and not have that marginalized and relegated to the realm of emotion? i challenge you to see my lived experience as theoretical production, theory as a mode of resistance from my specific location or position...and how do i teach from a blood space, a bone space? i crave to remain unmasked, raw, heart exposed...and i look at you and i am reminded of entitlement, privilege seeping deep, i envied your ability to put your experience at the center in every situation...i saw in you the reasons why my presence in academia is without rest...yet we came together...promising, as Adrienne Rich says, to go that long hard way together...when we committed to the creation of this learning community i am not sure we envisioned the depths to which this would push us against each other's reality...i remember telling you we would have to do together what we were asking our students to do...to negotiate the space of our differences...education for social justice...how we pushed against each other...attempting to create a space to make meaning of the multiple spaces of oppressions across our different race, culture, ethnicity, and class place...through my tears you seemed so far away...our lived experience so far away from each other's...it would have been so much easier to rest on the surface and yet for me and you impossible...and where did i struggle? i struggled to trust...i struggled to believe you would stay during the times of discomfort when you could so easily walk away and your place in this world would not be changed...i witnessed you contract...white liberalism tasted sour against my xicana/india tongue...

and my belly is swollen, ready to give birth, all that i learned germinating pushing against pelvis...waiting for the moment...embryonic fluid, rich clear milk of my body...release from these plump tissues what knowing has been constructed...i will hold it to my breasts...nurtured on the lives of my ancestors...i cannot and could not turn away and the deeper we worked the deeper our students engaged...i was witnessing a miracle and the power of education.

i have learned to find the crack in the armoring of my heart...i have learned to forgive...i have learned that i am not as assimilated as i thought...i learned that we must build strong partnerships, become strong allies if we are to create a culture of peace and nonviolence...and that it has to begin with us, you and me...for the seventh generation...i realize that my intensity is razor sharp and bone deep and i learned that people like me do not normally find themselves in the position i now walk...my presence and voice a constant reminder...and yes i live with a sense of urgency...this urgency born in a remembrance of my life before academia and my people's lives bending, as Gloria Anzaldúa says, under the hot sun...how dare i dream? how dare i not dream? i feel you were not prepared for all of who i am and my dear friend i thank you for not going away, or at least for coming back...and i thank you for coming to understand that bigger than you or me is the struggle for justice, for liberation, for democracy...my commitment to the struggle does not mean i disrespect you in any manner, but what it means is i will not compromise my commitment to the struggle for the liberation of my people and all people for your or my comfort...

i remember the day i read from the narratives of the wounded knee massacre...i had to pause, tears burning against the reality and the students many also unable to deny tears...they made the link in that moment...from the narrative which spoke to soldiers cutting the wombs out of las mujeres indias to the india teacher sitting in front of them...whom they had grown to love...in that moment they knew it was my/our/their wombs, it was my/our/their humanity...i thank you for giving us the space to go to those depths...i know this required a lot of trust from you...and i thank you for going that long hard way with me...you had to carry the weight/burden of a history of genocide, oppression, rape, hunger, torture against my people and other peoples of color that i placed on you...for my wounds are so close to the surface, the scabs oozing and when we collided i bled again, so easily and it was not you but what you represented to my lived experience...in order to work as intimately as this required i had to forgive, i had to forgive 500 years and not forget...gracias...for our struggle has carved out a space in my heart and in our students' hearts that can not be erased or made invisible...and this is how we change, poco a poco, in small ENORMOUS doable acts...

i offer this reflection with love, and respect for my teaching partner who had the courage and heart to go "that long hard way together" and to our courageous students who went with us. They are leaders towards a new vision where peace and democracy are a reality and possibility for all.

~ Deborah

As our letters to one another suggest, the importance of introducing concepts of privilege and power, the situatedness of any one perspective, and the nature of collaboration that may follow, cannot be overstated. As Adrienne Rich (1979) reminds us:

> An honorable human relationship—that is, one in which two people have the right to use the word "love"—is a process, delicate, violent, often terrifying to both persons involved, a process of refining the truths they can tell each other.
>
> It is important to do this because it breaks down human self-delusion and isolation.
>
> It is important to do this because in so doing we do justice to our own complexity.
>
> It is important to do this because we can count on so few people to go that hard way with us.

Our Learning Community

Our intention in designing *Education for Social Justice* was to create an opportunity for our students and ourselves to develop new knowledge about social justice and social change. We organized the curriculum so we could explore the social justice movement through the lenses of education and multicultural studies. We wrote in our syllabus that we would: explore the historical, socio-cultural, and philosophical foundations of education; explore concepts of race, class, gender, culture, power, and privilege and how these concepts play out in societal and educational settings; examine the relationship of critical issues in culture and education from our place, the local, to the global and back to the local; and work together to construct knowledge and engage in action to transform the conditions under which we live and realize our place in becoming active global citizens. We also let students know that their learning would be informed by reading and researching as well as by participating in a community-based project outside of class.

This project became a big component of the learning community. We shifted our language and practice from "service learning" to that of "community partnership" in order to challenge the baggage inherent in the notion of "service." Our students were required to spend a minimum of ten hours establishing a community partnership at a community agency with an educational mission. Central to this part of class was critical self-reflection. We posed several sets of questions to begin a dialogue on what it means to enter communities not our own from our privileged places. In order to help students reflect on their own cultural background, we used autobiography in an assignment called "mapping our personal geography," in which students brought in artifacts and wrote about their own cultural traditions. All quarter, students wrote journals and essays in which they connected their learning in class to their work in the community.

While students did this deep work, we paralleled what we asked our students to do, alone and together, including our critical self-reflections. Our work as teaching partners became increasingly powerful in shaping the experience within the learning community. We had to negotiate the space of race and class, and we had to have the courage to go "there" with each other.

As part of students' final project and portfolio, they had to demonstrate that they were able to:

- enter into a community-based partnership where all partners benefited from the experience;

- engage with and think critically about a social justice issue they felt passionately about, including researching the issue and becoming an agent for positive change within the community;
- discover how to take classroom/academic knowledge, make personal meaning of it, and apply it to their life and work;
- work both individually and with a group; and
- communicate their learning to others.

For the project, we asked students to work in groups of three or four, and select a site where they would each work at least one hour a week. Students attended an orientation at their sites and wrote a reflection based on that experience. Group members were to question each other and themselves about their expectations, fears, joys, and assumptions about the site prior to beginning work. The answers to these questions, the orientation materials, and the reflection on orientation became the first part of a portfolio due during the second week of the quarter.

Once students started working at the site, they were asked to keep a journal about their work, making observations and posing questions—including questions about assumptions, biases, and stereotypes at play in their own thinking, in their colleagues' thinking, or at the site itself. Students also kept a log documenting their attendance at the site. These journals, reflections, interrogations, and documentation of hours became the second part of their portfolio.

As students became more familiar with their community partner, they were asked to identify one social justice issue that was being played out at the site. They were to discuss the issue with their group members and in conference with one instructor, in order to make connections between what they were observing and what they were studying in class. Working on the Internet and with scholarly sources in the library, students were asked to write a group research paper providing background on the issue. Interviews with people in the community could be used as part of the data for the research paper, and groups were asked to give presentations about their issue near the end of the quarter.

The penultimate step of the project invited students to work with community partners to become agents for change, to put learning into action to make a positive difference. The project could take the form of a web site, zine, or video to inform the broader public. It could take the form of an action such as creating a dinner for the hungry in the community, developing a fund-raising idea, or organizing a demonstration. The main criteria were that it would put learning to use for the good of the community, that it be done in partnership with the community, and that students discuss it with the instructors before proceeding. Students were asked to document their work by writing about their own thinking, their group's process, and the community process. This reflection also became the basis for class presentations.

The final step in the process for students was to write a reflective essay focusing on what they learned, in particular on the ways their classroom-based work, their community-based work, and their group projects informed their learning overall. Students were asked to comment on how the experience had changed them, and on what they would take forward from this learning into their life and work.

We grounded our classroom practice in critical pedagogy and critical literacy theory based on the work of Paulo Freire, Antonia Darder, Henry Giroux, Ira Shor, and Peter McLaren. Critical pedagogy can be defined in many ways. For us, the definition that carries most weight is Giroux's idea that "pedagogy in the critical sense illuminates the relationship among knowledge, authority, and power" (Giroux 1994). In particular, Giroux notes that critical pedagogy exmaines how matters of audience, voice, power, and evaluation work to construct relations between teachers and students and between classrooms and communities. According to Darder (1991):

> Critical Pedagogy refers to an educational approach rooted in the tradition of critical theory. Critical educators perceive their primary function as emancipatory and their primary purpose as commitment to creating the conditions for students to learn skills, knowledge, and modes of inquiry that will allow them to examine critically the role that society has played in their self-formation. More specifically, critical pedagogy is designed to give students the tools to examine how society has functioned to shape and constrain their aspirations and goals, and prevent them from even dreaming about a life outside the one they presently know.

The required texts for the class were *Teaching to Change the World* (Oakes and Lipton 2002), *Teaching for Social Justice* (Ayers, Hunt, and Quinn 1998), and the compilation of articles, *Rethinking Our Classrooms, Vol. 1.*(Bigelow, et al., eds. 1994). Additional articles were placed on reserve for students. These texts were difficult for first-year college students, and our students had many questions, but they rose to the challenge. They didn't always agree with the perspectives of the authors and we had many lively classroom debates where students honed their critical thinking skills as they grappled with multiple perspectives.

We were able to reserve a large classroom for our learning community. We arranged tables and chairs in blocks toward the front of the room, and left an open space in the rear where we could easily bring our chairs into a circle or have an open space for our theatre of the oppressed work. Throughout the course we engaged the class in theatre of the oppressed activities using the work of Augusto Boal. We felt that moving away from the spoken word and allowing the body to speak might shift the dynamics of a predominately "white" classroom. We are always concerned when we begin the dialogues on "race" in a predominately "white" class, and we struggle with how to make the classroom space multi-centered so the students of color would not be made to feel obligated to act as "cultural informants." We found that using this work allowed all participants to feel safe expressing their thoughts and feelings while disrupting comfort zones. At particularly tough moments in the classroom we would pause and move into the theatre of the oppressed work, always finishing in a circle to process what we had just experienced.

The course was a very difficult one to teach and the letters that we wrote to each other attest to some of the struggles that we faced in trying to unravel the subtle strands of power and privilege that exist between and among us. Nonetheless, no doubt because of these struggles, the course was meaningful to both instructors and students at a very deep level. The students taking our class were primarily younger students who came to our community college from the surrounding suburbs. Most of them had attended suburban schools and most of them were white. They had read about injustice but for most of them, injustice was far removed from their experience. For their community-based learning, our students partnered with a number of different community agencies and most were interacting with children from the Mexican immigrant and/or refugee community.

Through this community partnership, the students were given the opportunity to see injustice in a way that many of them had never seen it before. For example, one of the agencies we worked with was attempting to develop an after-school program for parents and children in the immigrant community. They were offering after-school activities and tutoring in an apartment complex where many Mexican immigrant and/or refugee families lived, using the apartment recreation center as physical space to house the program (with permission from the apartment manager). Midway through the quarter, the apartment manager told the Americorps volunteers who were spearheading the project that they could no longer use the recreation center and would have to rent an apartment if they wanted to continue an onsite program.

It might be helpful to put this situation in context for the reader. The demographics in this affluent, suburban, high-tech corridor in northeast King County, outside of Seattle, Washington, have been changing dramatically. The immigrant and/or refugee populations have increased at a fast rate, and with the changing demographics comes the resistance of the predominately white community to accept the "browning of the community." The immigrant and/or refugee community here often faces exploitation, tenants' rights violations, racism, poverty, and more. By the time the programs were shut down our students who were working at the site had developed relationships with the families and were given the opportunity to witness an experience of the families they had grown to love, many of whom felt too vulnerable to protest the decision even though they were paying rent which ostensibly included access to the recreation center. We will never forget this group of students presenting what had happened to the class, many of them in tears, asking their classmates how we could raise money to rent an apartment so that the after-school program could be saved. For us, this was a moment where the distance between the students' privileged place and the reality of the lived experiences of the people the students had grown to love was shattered. We knew in that moment that they would be changed deeply and would not be able to go back to "I did not know"; it is in these moments, when we are educated for liberation. It is not enough for us to remain in the abstract space of academia. In creating partnerships with multiple communities, students can actually witness how people's lives and their own are affected by the systems and institutions that we often participate in without questioning their effects, both locally and globally.

When we received our student evaluations at the end of the quarter, they provided evidence of the growth our students had experienced. Twenty-nine of the forty-six students completed the evaluations. On the numerical ratings, students were very generous, giving us an average score of 4.95 out of a possible 5.0 ratings. In answer to the question, "What supported your learning?," students' written comments spoke to the meaning of the class for them:

> This is the most amazing class I've ever been in! My level of critical thinking and social justice has deepened so much. The issues were important.

> The class allowed us to think critically about topics and broadened points of view that are not looked at in our society.
>
> This class is a model demonstration of Cascadia's learning outcomes. We as students were part of the teaching and critical pedagogy.
>
> Diversity of teaching styles made coming to class a pleasure. Having both linear and random teachers, especially these two, gave me the opportunity to work in and out of my comfort zone which provided a challenge to me and kept me motivated.
>
> This course helped me understand this school's learning outcomes and the intentions behind them. This was the best learning environment I have ever participated in. I am so thankful to have had these teachers.
>
> Interacting in classroom discussions, hearing multiple points of view, getting first-hand experiences, textbooks, papers, handouts, other groups' presentations, and the open-minded support of teachers was great.

When asked what interfered with learning, there were fifteen brief comments including statements like these:

> Some people in the class are close-minded.
>
> The quarter was too short. This class should have another level.
>
> Where do we turn with questions when you are not around?
>
> Not every viewpoint is considered in the course materials.

Students who participated in our learning community continue to grow. Several students attended the international *Pedagogy and Theatre of the Oppressed* conference and presented with Debora. Other students participated in a project building houses for families in Tijuana, Mexico. One of the students has gone on to pursue a social work degree. Several have begun to work on their teaching degrees. One has been actively involved in border issues with friends outside of San Diego, California, and another has changed her major to a human rights interdisciplinary degree. Two students continued to work with Debora for a year after the class in a family literacy project.

As for us, we continue to be in awe of the power of emancipatory education. We take away the knowledge that something important happened in this class, for us and for our students. If we were to teach the same class again, there is no guarantee that we would get the same magical results. However, the fact that this can happen gives us hope. It is not easy to teach about oppression, power, and privilege to students who have rarely experienced injustice first-hand. It is not easy to do this when only a small number of students in class have intimately experienced oppression, poverty, racism, or exploitation. How do we negotiate the space of this classroom in such a way that all members retain their dignity and integrity? How do we negotiate the space of our class in a manner where we do not sanitize or diminish people's struggle for the sake of order in the classroom? As Darder (1991) asks us: "Do we dare use the word love?"

Many times in courses that attempt to confront issues of race, class, power, and privilege, students engage with the topics superficially, sometimes feeling that they are being "blamed" for a history of oppression, and generally resisting going to a deep level of understanding that might lead them to change their hearts. We were blessed in this experience to see what happens when students cease resisting. They did not all agree with our perspective, and if they had, that would be worrisome. What they did, almost universally, was to open their hearts. The last day of the quarter we sat in a circle and each shared what the course had meant to us. There were few dry eyes in the room. We watched young women as well as young men break down and cry about the injustice in the world that they had been blind to for most of their lives. We listened as they told us how they wanted to make a difference in the world. We listened as they spoke of their understanding about how they have benefited from others' exploitation and we listened as they spoke of their critique of their own comfort and luxury at the expense of others. Together we moved towards a literacy of power and community. What a tremendous gift. This is why we teach and this is why teaching is the strongest political act we can engage in at this moment in our history. Emancipatory education! Education for Liberation! Si Se Puede!

References

Ayers, W., J. A. Hunt, and T. Quinn, eds. 1998. *Teaching for Social Justice.* New York: The New Press and Teachers College Press.

Bigelow, B., L. Christensen, S. Karp, B. Miner, and B. Peterson, eds. 1994. *Rethinking Our Classrooms, Vol. 1.* Rethinking Schools, Ltd.

Darder, A. 1991. *Culture and Power in the Classroom*, Westport, CT: Bergin and Garvey.

Freire, P. 1973. *Education for Critical Consciousness*. New York: Continum.

Friere, P., and I. Shor. 1987. *A Pedagogy of Liberation: Dialogues on Transforming Education*. Westport, CT: Bergin & Garvey.

Giroux, H. A. 1994. *Disturbing Pleasures: Learning Popular Culture*. New York: Routledge.

McLaren, P. 2003. *Life in Schools: An Introduction to Critical Pedagogy in the Foundations in Education.* Boston, MA: Pearson Education.

Oakes, J., and M. Lipton. 2002. *Teaching to Change the World, 2nd Ed.* Boston, MA: McGraw Hill College.

Rich, A. 1979. *On Lies, Secrets, and Silence*. New York: W. W. Norton and Company, Inc.

Debora Barrera Pontillo is a full-time faculty member at Cascadia Community College, teaching courses focused on education, theater, and social change. Catherine Crain is a full-time faculty member at Cascadia Community College, teaching courses in psychology and education.

"Varying Realities of the Human Experience": University Studies Program at Portland State University

Charles Ryan Brown, Grace L. Dillon, Celine Fitzmaurice, Greg Jacob, Yves Labissiere, Antonia Levi, Cherry Muhanji, Candyce Reynolds, and Jack Straton

Like many institutions of higher education, Portland State University (PSU) has engaged in initiatives to promote a more equitable and democratic society, from curricular changes to institutional policy implementation. In the late 1980s, PSU required students to complete a certain number of "diversity" credits as part of its general education requirements. During the 1990s, PSU radically revised its approach to general education, creating the University Studies Program that places diversity awareness among its core goals. Most recently, current President Daniel O. Bernstine has instituted a comprehensive "Diversity Initiative" as part of a series of initiatives aimed at improving the quality of university life for students, faculty, and staff.

This paper recounts the institutional context for the University Studies Program's emphasis on diversity, provides an overview of the University Studies general education curriculum, which is designed as a series of interdisciplinary learning communities, and offers examples of teaching approaches that promote diversity awareness.

Institutional Context: PSU's Diversity Initiative

Institutional planning and resource allocation at PSU are guided by a series of Presidential Initiatives aimed at measuring and enhancing the quality of student, faculty, and staff experiences as members of our campus community. These initiatives emerged from the work of the Commission on Campus Climate and Life, a team appointed by President Bernstine in January 1998. The Commission focused primarily on the student experience and considered a broad range of questions, including obvious concerns such as whether library and technology resources adequately support learning, as well as larger issues related to students' social well-being. Based on the results of the Commission's 1999 Report, President Bernstine appointed Action

Councils for three initiatives: Diversity, Student Advising, and Assessment. (A fourth initiative, Internationalization, was added later.) These Action Councils were charged with more fully articulating goals and recommendations related to the initiatives.

PSU defines its identity as an urban university committed to partnering with constituents in the local community in order to create a better place to live and work. As the only urban university in the state, it serves the population of the Portland, Oregon-Vancouver, Washington, metropolitan area consisting of six counties of mixed urban and rural character. Ethnically this region is not very diverse. Census figures from 2000 show that 84.5 percent of the population is white. Since PSU is located in the heart of the downtown district of the largest and most diverse city in the region, it is no wonder that the process of institutional self-reflection identified diversity as a critical component of our commitment to serve the city. As the President's website points out, "PSU recognizes that diversity in faculty, staff, and student populations enriches the educational experience, promotes personal growth, strengthens communities and the workplace, and enhances an individual's personal and professional opportunities. As a public university, we have a special responsibility to work for equity and social justice and to make our programs truly accessible to our diverse constituents."[1]

In 1999, the Diversity Action Council (DAC) set about creating an Action Plan for increasing diversity of students, faculty, and staff. The DAC regularly advises the president and provost on relevant issues, works collaboratively with departments and programs throughout the university to ensure that curriculum includes diversity awareness, facilitates scholarship and research on diversity, and lobbies for resources in support of the Initiative. Goals in the Action Plan include increasing the number of students, faculty, classified staff, and administration from underrepresented groups and strengthening ties with regional communities that represent diverse populations. In keeping with the spirit of respecting multiple approaches and opinions, DAC's Action Plan paints its recommendations broadly while inviting individual units to determine the best means of implementing them. DAC regularly offers assistance to individuals, programs, and departments that seek help in making diversity a priority. Among its many activities, DAC oversees the production of a quarterly campus newsletter on diversity issues and works with the Center for Academic Excellence to award faculty and student mini-grants (up to $1,000) in support of proposals to fund curricular development and scholarship.

Projects funded by these grants have assessed the effectiveness of one faculty member's interracial dialogue workshop, helped another create a series of one- to three-minute computer video clips that European American faculty can use to bring the voices of people of color into their classrooms, and supported a website for students around the world to share stories of how they have intervened across racial lines.[2]

DAC also facilitates a "Focus on Diversity Series" showcasing faculty research related to diversity. The series theme in winter 2004 served to mark the 150th anniversary of Japanese-U.S. relations and included topics such as "The Myth of Japanese American Sabotage at Pearl Harbor & the Internment of U.S. Citizens" and "Challenges for Japan: A U.S. Perspective." DAC continues to monitor the university's progress and reports that in the last four years PSU's percentage of diverse faculty has risen from 6 percent to 13 percent; our percentage of undergraduate students from underrepresented groups has increased by 45.1 percent, which is 3.7 percent greater than the overall growth of the undergraduate population; and our percentage of graduate students from underrepresented groups has increased by 46.1 percent, which is 31.9 percent greater than overall graduate enrollment growth.

Diversity and the Emergence of University Studies

Faculty and administrators were encouraging institutional growth in diversity awareness well before the 1999 Report of the Commission on Campus Climate and Life suggested a Diversity Initiative. In 1993, a working group of faculty at PSU began examining its general education requirements and took on the question posed by then Provost Michael Reardon, "Can you state with conviction that these requirements are meaningful?" PSU's general education program at that time required students to take two diversity courses from an approved list of options distributed among different departments. By fall of 1992, 102 courses had been approved as satisfying the diversity requirement. The group working on general education reform appreciated that departments had an incentive to list as many courses as possible in order to maximize student credit hours, but also warned that the coherence and focus intended by the diversity requirement diminished as a consequence. Looking at the entire general education model, the group cited the need for improved academic preparation and for relevance and coherence throughout the curriculum. After much study of issues on campus and of general education nationwide, they proposed a new "University Studies" general education program that was approved by the Faculty Senate in late 1993.

The purpose of University Studies is to facilitate the acquisition of the knowledge, abilities, and attitudes that will form a foundation for lifelong learning among its students. Its four core learning goals are (1) inquiry and critical thinking, (2) communication, (3) awareness of the diversity of human experience, and (4) ethics and social responsibility. University Studies offers courses at all undergraduate levels and is a required program for incoming freshmen and for most transfer students. The yearlong foundation course, Freshman Inquiry, designed by interdisciplinary faculty teams, introduces students to all four program goals through thematic content. Following the Freshman Inquiry course, students elect three Sophomore Inquiry courses, each of which introduces them to a thematic cluster of upper-division courses. Students then elect to specialize in one area by taking three upper-division cluster courses in one theme. The final course is a Senior Capstone, in which interdisciplinary groups of students work with a faculty facilitator and a community partner to address needs and issues in the metropolitan region or beyond.[3]

Diversity awareness is integrated into the curriculum from Freshman Inquiry through Senior Capstone, and implementing diversity awareness as a goal to be threaded throughout all levels of the program challenges University Studies faculty to define diversity broadly. The latest iteration from the Freshman Inquiry Faculty Handbook (2003–04) is reproduced here:

The Freshman Inquiry student will understand and appreciate the varying realities of the human experience. This involves examining wider ethnic and cultural perspectives within the United States and around the world. Some of the issues connected may be those of class, race, gender, and sexual orientation. It also involves appreciating diverse beliefs, experiences, and forms of creativity entailed in the scientific, social, cultural, environmental, and artistic components of human experience; and an appreciation of how human diversity is fundamental to the full realization of human potential on an individual, community, and global level.

Rather than taking stand-alone courses on diversity issues that might lead students to isolate the concept of diversity as an intellectual construct separate from daily experience, PSU students encounter diversity issues throughout a four-year program of study that invites them to confront issues both theoretically and intimately, as they engage in real-world, community-based projects. The intention of this integration is to add relevance and coherence for students, elements that the working group found lacking in previous general education requirements as well as in their investigation of general education programs nationwide.

Laying the Foundation: Diversity in Freshman Inquiry

Freshman Inquiry courses are team-taught, multidisciplinary, yearlong courses. The themes have included: *Chaos and Community*; *The Columbia Basin*; *The Constructed Self*; *Einstein's Universe*; *Entering the Cyborg Millennium*; *Sex, Mind and the Mask*; *Forbidden Knowledge: The Sacred and the Profane*; *Meaning and Madness at the Margins*; *Metamorphosis*; *Pathways to Sustainability and Justice*; and *The Power of Place*. Three of these are also offered for seniors in four area high schools, with similar but extended curricula (see Traver, et al. 2003). The study of diversity enters into the storyline of each of these multidisciplinary courses in somewhat different ways, but it typically focuses on race and ethnicity and examines issues through the lenses of history, multicultural appreciation, and interpersonal and institutional oppression theory.

An extended example may help to demonstrate how issues of diversity arise naturally from the content of many of these Inquiry themes. *Columbia Basin Inquiry* focuses on the geographical region defined by the Columbia River, which is the second largest river by volume in the United States. Its watershed includes most of the surface area of Oregon, Washington, and Idaho, as well as portions of Nevada, Wyoming, Montana, Utah, and British Columbia. Portland, Oregon, is the largest city in the Columbia River Basin. Issues involving the Basin's economics, environment, and culture provide fodder for ongoing debates in the press and community. Through this course, students acquire an overview of the natural and human history of the Basin, examine the ethical, political, and social issues surrounding human/environmental interaction in the region, and make informed judgments about our stewardship of the region.

A number of opportunities exist for students enrolled in the *Columbia Basin Inquiry* to explore diversity issues, especially differences in ethnic and cultural perspectives, and differences in class and gender. An obvious topic is the natural economy of Native American tribes in the Columbia Basin. Most of our students are familiar with the industrial economy of the United States and its emphasis on fossil fuels, centralized production, and cash value. Students are less familiar with the Native American values for land and water. To Native Americans the landscape is organized into watersheds rather than cities and states, and the watersheds are interconnected rather than broken down into discrete economic spheres in the industrial economy (Fixico 2003). Salmon, for example, are not valued only after they are caught and processed. They are part of the natural cycle, and they provide necessary nutrients to the soil, insects, and wildlife after they have completed their life cycle. Students question and write about these two different economies, and they consider them from a perspective of land stewardship.

Students also have the opportunity to study the lives of people of color who have struggled to make a living in the Pacific Northwest. Students learn about Oregon public policy that segregated against African Americans; the unwritten but enforced policy that did not allow Chinese to fish commercially on the Columbia River, but instead gave them long working hours in the canneries as butchers; the dehumanizing treatment of Japanese citizens who were forced to relocation centers during WWII; and the economic and social struggles of the working class in Portland, Oregon, during the 1930s and 40s.

Another topic of diversity arises from examination of the treatment of women in Oregon during the nineteenth and early twentieth centuries. Women were often pigeonholed into categories such as schoolmarms, submissive housewives, and pistol-packing mamas. Students contextualize this depiction by reading and writing about the lives of Oregon women who would not accept the status quo and who would not accept sexist attitudes, including Tabitha Moffatt Brown, Abigail Scott Duniway, Bethenia Owens-Adair, Lola Greene Baldwin, and Alice Day Pratt.

Historical explorations of this sort are not unique to the C*olumbia Basin Inquiry* course. Other inquiries, for example, include nineteenth century anti-Semitism in Europe, European imperialism in Africa, eugenics, Jim Crow, and/or development of blues or jazz in the United States. Inquiry courses sometimes confront the topic of U.S. imperialism—for example, asking students to respond to the video *Hawaii's Last Queen* concerning the U.S.-backed overthrow of the constitutional government of Queen Liliuokalani and an article by Haunani-Kay Trask, "From a Native Daughter."

In considering the prominence of diversity awareness across Freshman Inquiry themes, it is important to note the cross-fertilization provided by integrating diversity awareness with other program goals. For example, faculty exploit the link between diversity studies and critical thinking in assigning Jane Tompkins' article "'Indians': Textualism, Morality, and the Problem of History," which confronts students, generally for the first time, with the notion that the perspectives we bring to an exploration of history are part of the history that we discover. A monthlong portion of the diversity module in winter term focuses intensively on the effects of racism in American culture. The connection to communication skills in a number of cases is provided by an article on group communication by Jack Straton (2004). A class might make a transition from history into the modern day by examining the idea that race is a cultural, rather than a biological, reality using articles like Michael Omi and Howard Winant's "Racial Formation" or the video *Race: The Power of an Illusion*. Within the modern era, diversity curricula typically explore both multicultural awareness and interlocking oppressions. The centerpiece for the former might include a film by Mina Shum that explores the bicultural challenges faced by a young woman growing up in a traditional Chinese family in Vancouver, B.C., *Double Happiness*, or *Smoke Signals*, about American Indians from the Coeur d'Alene nation in Idaho.

We generally move from the fascinating and intriguing facet of diversity awareness (learning about other cultures) into the other facet, which may be described as discovering and taking some responsibility for the ways in which dominant American culture has dealt oppressively with "other" ethnicities over time. This exploration involves readings about the reality of living with that oppression, such as Ronald Takaki's *A Different Mirror*, as well as workshops developed by University Studies faculty, like Cherry Muhanji's "Interlocking Oppressions," "The Race," "The Walk Around," and "Eye to Eye." These hands-on activities increase students' awareness that diversity has to do with more than race. In "The Walk Around," for example, Professor Muhanji (a woman) asks a female student to stand up, then takes her by the hand and walks around the room. When she nears two male students who are sitting next to each other, she drops the female's hand and asks for the hand of one of the males. He consents primarily because the social relationship being enacted demonstrates heterosexism. Professor Muhanji quickly picks up the other male's hand and presses it into the student's hand she was just holding. The students typically react with complete consternation, and discussion ensues on the topics of heterosexual privilege and homophobia. Comparable faculty workshops include "White Guilt" developed by Straton in collaboration with his off-campus colleague Lauren Nile. The centerpiece of this workshop is the video *The Color of Fear*, in which nine men of various ethnicities talk about their own experiences of race relations. Class sessions utilizing this film are detailed in chapters by Nile and Straton, Ross, and Straton in the forthcoming *The Color of Fear Sourcebook*.

Follow-up student workshops on some of the sticky points may include sessions on "Multiple Ways Institutions Reinforce Prejudice," "Wave-particle Duality and Affirmative Action," or "White Bashing." Much of the above curricula focuses on the need to help European American students examine the assumptions they bring to the classroom. This is of benefit to students of color in that it validates some of their experiences, lessens the burden on them to educate their European American peers, and provides more basis for genuine (reality-based) relationships. However, keeping such a disproportionate focus on European Americans, whatever the motivation, itself perpetuates the racist attitude that European Americans are to be subjects and all others are to be secondary objects. Consequently, some university faculty recently have begun including workshops focused specifically on the direct needs of students of color, particularly in dealing with what Nile calls "the daily indignities," the relentless episodes of mistreatment that people of color are subjected to by shopkeepers, police, airline agents, and others in the commercial sphere.

Complementing such student workshop activities are peer mentor classes—break-out companion sessions to the main class that bring together smaller cohorts of students for shorter meetings. On the issue of race, peer mentors (upper-division undergraduates whose role resembles that of teaching assistants in traditional departments) often present two different developmental perspectives to their students to help them understand how and why people deal with race and racism in the ways they do. Mentors discuss Rita Hardiman and Bailey Jackson's "Racial Identity Development: Understanding Racial Dynamics in College Classrooms and on Campus" (1992), which provides a model for understanding how racial identity is formed, and Beverly Tatum's "Talking About Race, Learning About Racism: The Application of Racial Identity Development Theory in the Classroom" (1996), which advances two theories of white and black identity development.

Peer mentors receive teaching materials that include resources for facilitating difficult discussions, materials for developing a well-rounded social identity for understanding systems of oppression, and articles that can be used to introduce students to new ideas about diversity, such as "White Privilege: Unpacking the Invisible Knapsack" by Peggy McIntosh. As a product of their ongoing training, mentors have constructed a "Diversity Binder." Mentors are encouraged to add to its contents when they discover or invent a successful diversity training exercise or source.[4]

Subsequent mentor contributions to diversity education at PSU came out of mentor development team meetings during the winter of 2003. A group of mentors established a series of workshops that addressed topics such as strategies for incorporating diversity issues into the curriculum in an organic way so they do not draw attention to them as "add-ons," outside the "content" of the course, and strategies for enhancing the experiences of diverse students, in particular older, returning students who do not fit the eighteen- to twenty-year-old profile of the majority of freshmen.

The culminating projects for the Freshman Inquiry diversity curricula may involve further research, reflective essays, or assignments that connected with the social responsibility theme of University Studies utilizing community-based learning projects. Perhaps the most useful end-project for assessment purposes is the three-term portfolio, which showcases multiple projects students have produced over the entire freshman year. Faculty collectively score these end-of-year portfolios using rubrics encompasing all four University Studies goals. The "Diversity of Human Experience Rubric" is provided here:

6 (highest) Portfolio creatively and comprehensively demonstrates an understanding of personal, institutional, and ideological issues surrounding diversity in a scholarly fashion, using concrete examples. The work reflects an ability to view issues from multiple perspectives, to question what is being taught, and to construct independent meaning and interpretations. Demonstrates broad awareness of how the self appears from the greater perspective of human experience, questions own views in light of this awareness, and contemplates implications for life choices in the personal and public spheres.

5 Portfolio presents persuasive arguments about, and insights into, prominent issues surrounding diversity, and discusses ways in which personal and cultural experiences influence lives, ideas, and events. Reflects on personal experiences within the broader context of human experience, demonstrating a sophisticated awareness of the limitations of subjective experience and an informed view of the role difference plays in societies and institutions.

4 Portfolio analyzes some issue(s) surrounding diversity, and demonstrates an ability to understand particular situations in the context of current concepts and theory. Discusses personal experience within the broader context of human experience, demonstrating a working knowledge of features of diverse peoples, societies and institutions, and analyzes these features in some way.

3 Portfolio demonstrates a basic working knowledge of central theories and concepts related to the study of diversity. Demonstrates some attempt to meaningfully locate oneself within the broader context of diverse culture.

2 Portfolio demonstrates a basic comprehension of some issues surrounding diversity, but refers only in a limited way to current theory and concepts. Relates personal experiences within the context of broader human experiences, but does not locate self within that context in a thoughtful manner.

1 (lowest) Portfolio uses some terminology surrounding diversity, but fails to demonstrate meaningful comprehension of key concepts.Tells of personal experiences but does not connect, compare or contrast those with the experiences of others.

Building Knowledge and Experience: Diversity in Sophomore Inquiry, Junior Clusters, and Senior Capstones

Sophomore Inquiry courses span some thirty offerings from *The Nineteenth Century: Revolution and Evolution* to *Natural Science Inquiry*. While Inquiries such as African Studies and Women's Studies naturally have strong diversity components, other courses also include a significant diversity focus. For instance, *Popular Culture*, which includes a discussion of race representation on television using Michael Omi's article, "In Living Color: Race and American Culture," and Robert Entman and Andrew Rojecki's *The Black Image in the White Mind: Media and Race in America*. Students in *Popular Culture* are introduced to cultural imperialism through Sherif Hetata's article, "Dollarization, Fragmentation, and God," as well as to material about gender images in the media, African American influences in music, images of Latin America in film, and an African American critique of European American intellectual pursuits of postmodernism.

Each Sophomore Inquiry course is a gateway to an Upper Division cluster. Once students emerge from Sophomore Inquiry into the junior year, they align a series of cluster courses with the inquiry theme of their choice. There are numerous cluster courses available representing the disciplines of several departments. The *Popular Culture* cluster, for example, includes literature courses on science fiction, music courses on jazz history, theater arts courses on media and culture, urban studies courses on information cities, and anthropology courses on folklore. In order to align offerings with a cluster, departments must demonstrate that the course incorporates the University Studies goals, thereby ensuring continuity throughout the curriculum. The presence of diversity awareness, like the other core goals, therefore remains throughout the junior year.

The culmination of the University Studies Program is the capstone requirement. This community-based learning course is designed to provide students with the opportunity to apply, in a team context, what they have learned in the major and in their other University Studies courses to a real challenge emanating from the metropolitan community. Interdisciplinary teams of students address these real challenges and produce a final product under the guidance of a PSU faculty member.

The capstone's purpose is to further enhance student learning by cultivating crucial life abilities that are important both academically and professionally, including establishing connections within the larger community, developing strategies for analyzing and addressing problems, and to working with people trained in fields different from one's own. Capstone offerings include such topics as prevention of domestic and school violence; grantmaking with community organizations; creative industries: student ad agency; history inquiry in the context of Lewis and Clark; homelessness & poverty capstone; and many others.

Capstones that naturally involve issues of diversity include, for example, working with and beside students and faculty of the Chemawa Indian School in creating a documentary research project that combines visual art and first-person narratives exploring Native American community life and culture in the Pacific Northwest. This capstone engages students in examining the importance of identity, place, community, culture, and community building. Students then incorporate theory with community experience to document the voices of Chemawa students, members of the Native American community and their ancestors, providing educators with projects, photographs, narratives, and themes that can be integrated into their own curricula.

Specific lessons designed to promote diversity awareness in capstone courses are varied but continue promoting techniques of reflection. In *Middle School Science and History in the Context of Lewis & Clark*, for example, community partners are teams of middle school students engaged in informal science and history inquiry activities inspired by the Lewis and Clark Expedition. The program is designed to help middle school students "rediscover" the flora, fauna, landscape, and histories of indigenous populations of the lower Columbia River Basin. Capstone students assist adult instructors as they direct their own students' science and history research projects.

Some capstone instructors use a reflective writing assignment on socioeconomic diversity, illustrating once again the broadly based approach to defining "diversity" that is central to the University Studies goal. Sociologists have identified sets of skills and knowledge called cultural capital that helps an individual "navigate the system"—have their interests and needs attended to. Studies suggest that people from low socioeconomic status (SES)—a social class of an individual based on income—have less cultural capital than do middle- or upper-income groups and that, as a consequence, low SES groups are discriminated against in the allocation of resources and benefits. Capstone students write responses to questions regarding the presence of class discrimination in the United States, focusing on the impact of SES on the likelihood of youths' development into successful adults.

Final Reflections: Assessing Diversity Awareness

The assessment process with regard to diversity begins with a prior learning survey. Its purpose is to capture a sense of who our students are at the beginning of the academic year so that we may incorporate diversity issues relevant to their own experiences. The survey measures such variables as student perception of their race and ethnicity, class background, skills, primary concerns, hopes, academic aspirations, and family education background. The entire dataset (without any variable that may identify an individual student) is made available to administrators, faculty, staff, and students themselves within two weeks from the start of the academic year. Faculty may share the survey data with students as a means of introducing the topic of diversity or to modify or supplement their syllabi. Administrators have used the data to develop advising programs that address specific student needs, such as first-generation college students and returning students. At the end of the academic year, we conduct a follow-up questionnaire to gauge student experience and assess retention issues. This data is collected so we can identify systemic concerns and issues that particular groups of students may face.

We also track progress within the curriculum using our diversity awareness goal as a touchstone. The third-term portfolio rubric on diversity provided earlier in this article went through many drafts in yearlong conversations that challenged faculty to clarify exactly what we mean by "diversity on campus." The assessment process engages faculty in useful discussions about how to operationalize diversity in our classes. Early in the program, for example, student scores on the diversity rubric were low. As a result, program administrators identified diversity as the priority goal for the following year. Development activities included bringing guest speakers to campus, inviting faculty to informal "brown bag" discussions, recalibrating our community-based learning conversations, conducting workshops, constructing a website of diversity resources, and developing specific learning modules on diversity. At the end of that year, diversity scores on the third-term portfolio were up. When they dropped several years later, we again revisited the rubric and resumed an emphasis on diversity as part of the ongoing assessment cycle.

The assessment questions we pose ask students to evaluate their experiences acquiring skills in working with others as a member of a team; exploring issues of diversity such as race, class, gender, sexual orientation, and ethnicity; and exploring ethical issues. The assessment results of the prior year are shared with faculty at a fall retreat. Faculty teams then discuss how we will address particular lacunae in the syllabi and curriculum that may improve student performance on this goal.[5]

Recent assessment results are promising with regard to the diversity awareness goal. For example, when asked which skills they employed to accomplish their community-based learning project, 84 percent of students indicated "Working with others of different cultural, racial, ethnic, and religious background." When asked which University Studies goal their community-based learning project most connected to, 43 percent indicated the diversity goal. By renewing our commitment to promoting diversity awareness through an ongoing assessment process, the University Studies Program works to ensure that PSU's institutional values and objectives are being realized.

Endnotes

1. http://www.president.pdx.edu.

2. The Racial Intervention Story Exchange (RISE): http://rise.pdx.edu/index.html.

3.http://www.ous.pdx.edu.
4.Diversity materials are available on a mentor's resource page at http://www.unst.mentor.pdx.edu.
5.Work samples and reflections from the third-term portfolio process are available at http://cyborglab.pdx.edu/portfolioproject.

References

Fixico, D. L. 2003. *The American Indian Mind in a Linear World: American Indian Studies and Traditional Knowledge*. New York: Routledge.

Hardiman, R., and B. Jackson. 1992. "Racial Identity Development: Understanding Racial Dynamics in College Classrooms and On Campus." *New Directions for Teaching and Learning* 52, 21–37.

Nile, L. N., and J. C. Straton. Forthcoming. "How to Deal with the Guilt that Results from Societal Racism." In *The Color of Fear Sourcebook*, edited by H. Vasquez and V. Lewis.

Ross, J. Forthcoming. "White Privilege and The Color of Fear." In *The Color of Fear Sourcebook*, edited by H. Vasquez and V. Lewis.

Straton, J. C. 2004. "Communicating in a Group." *Journal of Student Centered Learning*.

Straton, J. C. Forthcoming. "Imagining What They Mean." In *The Color of Fear Sourcebook*, edited by H. Vasquez and V. Lewis.

Straton, J. C. Forthcoming. "Converting Emotional Reactivity to Conscious Awareness." In *The Color of Fear Sourcebook*, edited by H. Vasquez and V. Lewis.

Tatum, B. D. 1996. "Talking about Race, Learning about Racism: The Application of Racial Identity Development Theory in the Classroom." In *Facing Racism in Education, 2nd ed,* edited by S. Anderson, P. Attwood, and L. Howard. Harvard Educational Review.

Traver, B., J. C. Straton, J. Whittlesey, D. Erhenkranz, T. Wells, P. McCreery, M. Paris, C. Reynolds, and J. Patton. 2003. "Senior Inquiry: A University/High School Collaboration." *Academic Exchange Quarterly* 7(3), 52–56.

Charles Ryan Brown is the program manager for the Professional Development Center at Portland State University.
Grace Dillon, Yves Labissiere, Cherry Muhanji, and Jack Straton are assistant professors in the University Studies Program at Portland State University.
Antonia Levi is an associate professor in University Studies.
Greg Jacob is an assistant professor of English at Portland State University.
Candyce Reynolds directs the mentor program in University Studies.
Celine Fitzmaurice is a service-learning instructor and youth program coordinator at Portland State University.

The Washington Center's National Learning Communities Project Monograph Series

Learning Communities in Community Colleges
Julia Fogarty and Lynn Dunlap with Edmund Dolan, Maria Hesse, Marybeth Mason, and Jacque Mott

Learning Communities in Liberal Arts Colleges
Karen Spear with J. David Arnold, Grant H. Cornwell, Eve Walsh Stoddard, Richard Guarasci, and Roberta S. Matthews

Integrating Learning Communities with Service-Learning
Jean MacGregor with Marie Eaton, Richard Guarasci, Maria Hesse, Gary Hodge, Ted Lewis, Marybeth Mason, Judith Patton, Lin Nelson, John O'Connor, Penny Pasque, and David Schoem

Learning Communities in Research Universities
John O'Connor with James A. Anderson, Jodi Levine Laufgraben, Karen Oates, David Schoem, Nancy S. Shapiro, and Barbara Leigh Smith

The Pedagogy of Possibilities: Developmental Education, College-Level Studies, and Learning Communities
Gillies Malnarich with Ben Sloan, Phyllis van Slyck, Pam Dusenberry, and Jan Swinton

Learning Community Research and Assessment: What We Know Now
Kathe Taylor with William Moore, Jean MacGregor, and Jerri Lindblad

Doing Learning Community Assessment: Five Campus Stories
Jean MacGregor with Michelle D. Cook, Lynn Dunlap, Shari Ellertson, Doug Epperson, Teresa L. Flateby, Mary E. Huba, Phil Jenks, Yves Labissiere, Jodi Levine Laufgraben, William S. Moore, Judy Patton, and Les Stanwood

Learning Communities and the Academic Library
Sarah Pederson

Learning Communities and Fiscal Reality: Optimizing Learning in a Time of Restricted Resources
Al Guskin, Mary Marcy, and Barbara Leigh Smith

Monographs may be ordered from:
The Evergreen State College Bookstore
2700 Evergreen Parkway NW
Olympia, WA 98505
360.867.5300
360.867.6793 (fax)